A Father's Love

Tabetha Henderson

TRILOGY CHRISTIAN PUBLISHERS

TUSTIN, CA

Dedication

*My Heavenly Father who has never left me nor
forsaken me.
Who has given me life's most significant purpose
to be called His very own,
My beloved Husband who has endured and loved
me endlessly through every valley and storm,
My beautiful children Jacob, Joshua, and Kylie
who have journeyed with me in discovering,
A Faithful Father's Love.
To all those that have been a part of this journey,
I pray you will see the reflection of His great love.*

Preface

In the springtime of 2019, I was working dili-
gently on a few projects. In the middle of the day,
I had an overwhelming feeling that I was to focus
on a particular assignment from the Lord; unsure
of what it was, I committed my heart to pray and
seek the Lord. But before I could even pray, that very
night, my eleven-year-old son Joshua said to me as
we were driving home from dinner, "Mom, you need
to write your testimony in a book and call it *A Father's Love*. My heart shook with awe and wonder because I knew it was the Lord giving me the direction
for the new assignment that had just begun. Joshua
did not know that I felt an urgency from the Lord,
that He was calling me to focus on a specific purpose from Him alone.

In all my years walking with the Lord, I had never
had such a clear direction; I knew without a shadow
of a doubt this was the Lord, and it was time to write
the book. Several years ago, in 2011, during a trying

season in my young Christian life, I asked the Lord why I was facing so many battles and why things always seemed to be an uphill climb for me. I cried out in anguish to Him, looking for the comfort of His love. He immediately revealed to me that I would write a book about my journey one day, and all I had endured would be a part of the story.

It was no surprise to me that Joshua said, "Mom, you need to write a book." It was something I knew deep in my heart for such a long time that I would one day record all the miraculous things the Lord has done for me. In the journey later in the pages, you will see a significant part about the two witnesses that led me to Christ. After I had encountered the miracle that changed my life, I would see these ladies here and there at conferences and such, and I would always say to them, one day I am going to write a book, and I am going to tell about your part in my story.

The significant part about Joshua prophesying this book into life is that it was in God's appointed time. It had been several years since I was born again, but the Lord had so much to teach me about life and His overcoming grace before I could start the journey of writing my story. This story was still being written, so at every page, at every new chapter, it was another season of my life that I had to discover the truth of a Father's love. This book couldn't have been written tens of years ago or even five years ago; it had to come at the appointed time.

The Lord didn't stop confirming His Word with my son Joshua, and I continued to encounter divine direction from the Lord. Several weeks after, Joshua spoke to me about this book. I was at a prayer meeting in the middle of the city. A woman of God whom I never met, came over to me and greeted me in the Lord with a beautiful hug. She prayed for me and said, "Honey, God has something very particular for you to do, an assignment just from Him! It is unique for you, and He said the doors would open when you obey Him and do what He said!" She proceeded to pray and said, "Nothing is missing, nothing is broken in you, dear!" I knew exactly what assignment the Lord was speaking about. Once again, I never had such clarity and direction for an appointed time. I always knew I would write someday, but the someday was now today.

During church one day, I went to the altar to seek My Father's love, looking for more of His presence, desiring His love to continue to change and comfort me. I love going to the altar; it was the place it all began with me. Seeking God with all my heart is the greatest joy and strength of my life. While at the altar, another beautiful sister in the Lord came to pray with me. She prayed and cried out with great urgency for me to "remember the book." I had not spoken this to her, and she had no knowledge that God had told me to write a book. Once again, God had confirmed His word.

Several weeks later, again, I went to the altar to pray, and the Lord, once again, sent the same sweet sister to pray for me, and say, "Don't forget the book."

After all these divine moments, I knew I needed to get to work. It was easier said than done. The journey began to write the book, and it was as if everything started to oppose me in my life. I faced yet another challenging season, with significant distress and opposition on every side. However, I knew God said, "You need to write the book." I could write a book about writing the book! Because it was another journey in learning how to overcome and truly press into all the Lord has called you to do.

At the height of the most challenging time of my life, I went again to the altar. This time it was different. We had a guest speaker that day, who knew nothing about me, or the book. I was facing some very trying situations that I was not sure how to handle. I went to the altar for prayer, and the guest speaker came to pray for me. While she was praying for me, she encouraged me that God was going to restore double of everything the enemy had stolen and that the Lord was anointing my head with oil in the presence of my enemies. She also encouraged me in my worship and said it was freeing to watch me freely dance before the Lord. The Lord was very aware of the trouble the enemy was causing me, and He ensured me that I would recover all, and I was His. But the prayer didn't end there. She proceeded to say, "Wait a minute, do you write? I feel like you write, and the Lord said to write the book!"

I felt the wind of the Spirit of God! I cried out with a loud cry, barely able to stand. Because I knew that God himself had ordained this work, and it was time to write the book. Anytime you are on an assignment from the Lord, the enemy will come and try to cause all kinds of distractions and troubles, but you can be sure that God's plan will never fail. Here is the book!

From the beginning to the end, He has given it all to me. This is my story, His story, one that will reflect His glory. He has revealed to me the depths of a Father's Love. As you turn through these pages, allow His love to speak to you as He did me. At every step of my life, it was another piece of the miraculous journey, a picture of a stain-glassed masterpiece that once was just merely broken pieces with no sense of purpose. It then joined and mended by

His love to reflect a Father's Love. This book is for everyone. It is my testimony of overcoming a life of great difficulty by the power of *A Father's Love* revealed in Jesus Christ. To God be all the Glory, for it is His love that has written my story.

CHAPTER 1

A Father's Love

When you think of a Father's love, what comes to your mind? How do you describe such an important foundational relationship between a father and a child? To be called a father, you have to be accountable for a child, or people following you. Some are fathers to children that they have adopted or may even be a father-like figure in children's hearts. A father is one that goes before us to pave a path of certainty. A father is a leader who first must know the way. A father produces more like himself and leaves an imprint of his reflection upon his children's hearts and minds that follow after him. A father is one that creates a child after his likeness. A father establishes peculiar people and calls them his very own. Rather by birth and blood, or adoption certified in courts, or by becoming a spiritual father to many, you may be leading along the journey of this life. A father establishes identity in the heart of the child or person. Every life is dependent upon the firm foundation of a father's love.

A skilled constructor knows that a house is only as strong as the foundation. Our lives are a lot like houses. We all need a foundation, a place to start. Without a father, there would be no life. No beginning. No birth. No purpose. Every life begins with the life of a Father. A father is a foundation that secures identity, purpose, provision, protection, direction, and loving correction. A father's role is vital to building a generation that will overcome and become pillars for generations to come.

IDENTITY

A father's love establishes identity in the life of a child. An identity gives the assurance of belonging. When you are born, you are entrusted into the arms that gave you life. Just think about a beautiful newborn baby, how joy fills the parent's hearts, the father and mother joined together, and created a child after their likeness. Does the child have their father's eyes and mother's hair? Will they grow to become strong and passionate like their father? A businessman, a teacher, will they grow into a life of service for others? From the moment the child is formed, their father's characteristics identify them. Even the physical characteristics are reflections of their father. The child was born and given a name that identifies them with their very own father. The beauty of the child just born is that the father has paved the way for his child and established a place for their newborn baby. The identity of the child is already marked by having their father's characteristics and name.

The child's name is forever documented on a birth certificate that verifies their name, parents, date, and place of birth. It is a legal document that secures your citizenship and privileges for the rest of your life. Without proper identification, you are not allowed or permitted access to many of life's necessities. In the heart of a child, identity is the security of belonging and access to provisions of being a son or daughter. Identity is a vital building block to purpose in a child's life, to which a father's love ensures unending love, acceptance, provision, and support.

PROVISION

A father establishes provisions for his child. He has prepared a home, a place of safety, a place of comfort to grow in. A place he can call home, a home he can run to when he needs rest. A place of nutrition where the child can replenish themselves physically, spiritually, mentally, and emotionally. A place of comfort. A place of compassion in their distress. A place of counsel and safety, knowing that their confidence is in the shelter of a loving father who desires to guide, correct, and nurture, who loves and provides. A home is a place of forgiveness, knowing that the father's love covers and protects, never castaways his children. A father's love is a place of refuge and strength. He provides all your needs from the physical home to the place you learn and grow, where your mistakes will never define you but align you to your father's love. Can you imagine the love of a father, the excitement of a child, and having a place specifically and uniquely designed for his child? Every detail was thought of, calculated, and prepared. Each aspect was carefully considered and designed for the child to have a place of provision and belonging, a sanctuary. All the child's needs, from having a place to sleep, food to eat, the comfort of shelter, a place to rest in safety, were all met and planned out by the father. A father commits to a life of providing: spiritually, physically, mentally, and emotionally for their children... no matter the cost. A father's love will not hold back one good thing in their child's life. He will give all he has to provide all that they need. A father's love keeps their children protected. He secures their home and takes all the safety precautions to protect what he values the most. A father will stand in the face of a threat to defend his family from all manners of harm. A father gives you priceless wisdom to keep you all the days of your life. He teaches you to obey and instructs you to keep you safe in all of your ways. A father not only protects you, but he also equips you and trains you to exercise wisdom in all you do. Providing a place for the child to come home establishes security in the heart of the child. The child does not wonder where his meal is coming from when his belly is hungry; a father provides every need of his child. A child does not have to wonder where he will lay his head down to rest at night. His loving father established his place of comfort and safety.

PURPOSE

The word "vision" is in the word provision. A father's love creates a perfect vision, a clear understanding, a perfect view. Scripture tells us without vision, the people perish. The vision comes from the father. Another way to explain vision is "purpose." I remember when my children were born, my husband looked at our first child as he laid in his bassinet with such awe and wonder; he gently held our son's hand and was amazed at his fingers. He said to me, "Do you see his hands? Look at how long his fingers are! He declared he is going to be a mechanic; he is going to be able to fix things." As Jacob grew, his mechanical gifting and craftsman ability grew right along with him. Jacob has great potential and has a lot to offer this world with the father's gifts in his life, but sure enough, my husband was correct, He is a craftsman, and that is wonderful! From the moment Jacob was born, his father spoke purpose over his life, knowing instantly that there would be a great craftsman's ability in our child.

When our second son, Joshua, arrived in this world is a day I will never forget. In the operating room, my husband was the first to lay eyes on our beautiful son. He said, "This boy is going to be a football player. Look at him! He is built like a ballplayer!" To my amazement, I looked over at my 9 pounds 2 ounces beautiful son, thinking he looked more like he was three months old! This child was born in strength and power. He had a call to endure and persevere and lead many. As you could guess, his first year in football season, the coach came to us and said, "Your son has a true gift to play ball, he has an amazing ability to tunnel vision out there, and that's what you need! If he keeps up with this, he will be a great ballplayer." Looking back, I could still hear my husband's words spoken over our son in the delivery room.

From the moment our children were born, their father saw a vision of who they would become. It is the most priceless treasured memory of a father's love; a father's love has a purpose for his children. My husband always encouraged our children to pursue their giftings. Jacob has had a toolset and musical instruments in his hand since day one. Joshua has been our sports guy and competitor, truly a gift of endurance. From the moment our sweet daughter Kylie was born we knew the Lord was going to use her vocally; she would sing. Today this little girl parades through the house with a song on her heart continually, she sings, and she sings beautifully! Vision, the father's love has a vision for his children, He knows their deep place of calling and belonging, and he makes the provisions so that each one of those callings can develop into great maturity.

Every person desire is to know and understand their unique significant purpose in life. They long to fulfill it. I genuinely believe that having confidence in your identity leads you to understand your purpose. A child who knows who they are will see what they are created for. A father's love will journey along with you through every valley and storm on the path of discovering the real purpose of your life. A father will continually reassure the child's heart on their secured identity and never fail to be a voice of hope. A father will freely give his child every opportunity to navigate their strengths and weaknesses to learn their virtues as they set out to fulfill their destiny. We discover our gifts and talents as we grow in our passions of purpose in life.

DIRECTION

A father provides the direction in the heart of the child. When growing up, regardless of what stage you are in, every child, whether an infant, toddler, adolescent, teenager, young adult, or even matured son needs direction. A father will always be there to provide direction in the child's life. A father's love won't lead a child astray or lead a child to fall. A father's love guides to keep that child on the best path possible for their lives. A father's love goes before the child and paves a path of certainty. A loving father does not want a child to face difficulties and hardships that could end in disaster, so they carefully guide the child through life with wisdom to ensure they have given their child the best direction possible to lead a life of success.

Have you ever had a time in your life that you needed direction? Real direction? To where you needed to make a difficult decision and needed to know the right way to go? An important decision, like leaving a position within a company or breaking off a relationship that isn't fruitful? Some decisions can be tough to make; some decisions you face can leave you with a no-win situation. In those very difficult decisions, we need a father's love of direction, and we need to be able to look and seek our father's wisdom and foresight. A father's love is the direction in every challenging place and situation. A father looks at your valley of decision in love and understanding, weighing out and truly providing the best for you in your direction. A true father will never leave you without the safety of trusted counselors, without the security of provision. He will guide and lead you every step of the way. But what is so beautiful is a father's love will always allow you to choose; he never forces his path, or plan or ideal on you. He prays and longs for you to choose the way he has provided, knowing it will ultimately lead you to the best life, but he will always give you the ability to choose freely. How beautiful is a father's love that provides us with the true direction in our lives? How beautiful is it to know a father goes before you and makes a place for you? That brings my heart so much comfort knowing that if my Father tells me this is the way to walk in it, I can confidently take that path, with assurance He has provided for me. Even when I may choose wrong, I love that a Father's direction is never removed or forgotten but is always ready to welcome and help correct that place of a wrong turn. A Father's love doesn't condemn us when we get lost along our way. It longs to restore us to get us back to the place of wholeness.

Every season, there is away. A father's love lights the path of direction. When a child is confident in the firm foundation of a father's love, they will never fail to know which way is the right way to go. A father's love gives you clear direction. Even though we will all have times of waiting, we will never have to wonder which path to take because our guide is always secured. A father's love doesn't keep you guessing but gives you confident assurance and leads you along the way to fulfill your unique purpose.

CORRECTION

A father's love understands and values correction. He will not allow his children to go astray. True love confronts you when you are taking the wrong path. Think about it. If you are on the road and there is danger ahead, a faithful father warns you to keep you safe. Correction is in the heart of a father's love. We know that receiving correction isn't easy, but we know in our hearts that it is vital and proves our Father's love for us. A child learns and grows in every season, discovering the challenges and obstacles in life that we all endure. Our loving fathers gently counsel us, impart unconditional love, wisdom, and encouragement as we continue on our course.

We seek counsel from our fathers to steer us in the right direction. They guide us through the difficult decisions of what schools to attend, what friendships to make, and even our desires to start our own families. When we find ourselves in the hard places of life with our dreams shattered and hearts broken, we run to our Father's house to find refuge. His love strengthens us, comforts us, and repairs us.

Our Father's house is our firm foundation, absolute safety, love, and protection. It's the place of true belonging and acceptance. We all desire to have a place to call home, a trusted counselor, safe arms of provision and direction. We want someone to watch over us and patiently guide us through every stage in this life. Then one day, we will become a reflection of a father's love and pass down that same foundational truth to the generations to come.

A father's love is a rich place of unfailing trust and priceless comfort. It is a secure identity, purpose, provision, protection, direction, and loving correction. The heart of every child is truly complete when they know the safety of the Father's love. When your house is built on a firm foundation, you can be sure that your home will stand. A father's love will never fail to repair what has been broken, provide what is needed, protect, and guide you into every path and season of this life.

My journey of understanding and discovering a true father's love came through many valleys and storms, wrong roads and turns, and an endless pursuit of finding identity and purpose in this fallen world. This book is a walkthrough of my miraculous journey of discovering the truth of a father's love.

CHAPTER 2

Who is My Father?

THE FATHERLESS

A life built upon the foundation of a father's love is secured in the pillars of identity, purpose, provision, protection, direction, and correction. Now knowing the vital importance of being rooted in the foundation of a father's love, can you imagine the heart of the fatherless? We are all created equal but unique in nature and design. However, we all are made with the same primary structure. Not one person is born without the inner needs of development that come in the comfort of true love and endless support of a father.

The hearts of the fatherless have desperate cries and pleas. The longing for love and acceptance. A place of true belonging. Their deep insecurities and desires to belong in the arms of their Father's where their life began. Can you imagine the brokenness and despair? The cry of loneliness and need for repair? The search for identity and purpose? We witness it everywhere, a fatherless generation. They search to find a place that has a purpose for them. They feel lost and without direction, unloved, and rejected. They have no security or provision. Acceptance will easily influence them, and they will go where they feel valued and affirmed.

The fatherless have to adapt quickly in this world to attempt to overcome the void in their lives. They find insurance in achievement and acceptance; they are searching for true identity. Some find purpose in a life of overachieving. They strive to obtain all the successes this world has to offer. Perfection is their companion. One place of achievement after another... filling their lives with more and more with hopes to fill the void of abandonment in their souls. When they run out of strength and accomplishments to conquer or their friends abandon them, they are left alone and empty. Staring into the mirror of "what have I become" and "why isn't my attempt to be 'perfect' satisfying my life, as I hoped it would become?" All along, they have buried the longings deeply for a father's love under their attempts to find perfection in what they have achieved. Their heart's cry is found in the father's love, unconditional acceptance, not based on accomplishments, but simply because they are completely loved.

Some search so far and wide for acceptance that they adventure onto the roads of rebellion. No one ever woke up and just decided that today would be the day they would give their lives away to drug addiction. It does not happen like that. Their hearts are wandering and searching for a cure to the emptiness they feel within. They did not find it in success or achievements. They instead found a group of friends that struggle with the same conditions. They find comfort in one another and try to cover the pain by one high after another. They go on a self-destructive path, not realizing the real void inside is looking for a true love that will satisfy them. They want help but do not know how to untangle the web of lies that not only filled their souls but now what their bodies are dependent on too. Their minds battle anxiety and depression, so the only way to stop the noise is to numb and suppress the loneliness of emotions that afflicts their souls. They are hurting so profoundly with a pain that only the love of a father can mend. They need correction and direction, forgiveness, and grace. They need strength and encouragement; they need a love that brings perfect restoration. They are crying out, "can anyone help me? Does someone hold the key?" Family members and loved ones may send them to rehab for a cure, but that cure they need is more significant than a program. It's their souls that need to be restored, to repair the broken foundations of their lives.

The fatherless heart is a place of deep abandonment, insecurities, brokenness, helplessness, and severe identity issues. We sometimes are quick to judge by looking outside, not understanding that we all have the same obstacles to overcome. We all have places of pain and injustice. We all long for the same true love of a father. We may not all respond the same, but the root remains, and healing is something we all need. Every life needs the pillars to lean upon. When there are missing pieces and no father, you have a people with broken foundations, wounded souls, and a cry to be restored to a truly loving father.

Without a father's love, we have no real identity. With no identity, no purpose, no direction, no correction... that will lead you to a place of wandering and destructive devastation. With no proper foundation, pillars cannot stand. The foundation of life determines your success, and real success in life can only be defined by fulfilling your unique purpose that you were created for by a father's love. The only right foundation that will stand is knowing a father's love and building your life upon the pillars of his loving care.

BORN INTO ABANDONMENT

Ever since I was a young child, I had an overwhelming desire to know my father. My father abandoned me when I was just an infant. I remember hearing the stories about my childhood. My family would say, "Tabby, all you did was scream for the first six months of your life." We never knew what was wrong with you, but you never slept, you cried nonstop for the first six months of your life, you were never happy. I was told that I was angry and rebellious in my toddler stage. My grandmother took me to Disney world around the age of three, and she said, "You threw a fit so bad you ripped the plastic interior off of the inside of my car, we couldn't get you to calm down." They said I was just miserable, unhappy, angry, stubborn, and they never knew how to handle the brokenness in my soul.

As young as an infant and born into this life, having a wound so deep that only God could see. I couldn't imagine any child born with a broken heart, but I genuinely believe that child was me. Every child longs for a Father, and when my father left me even as an infant, I think it was the first wound to my young soul that could not understand the deep cries and longing of my heart to be held in the arms of my father. We all have a story, we are all born into this life, and we all have to endure some level of pain that is deep inside. This is just my story, and like everyone else, my story starts on the day I was born. I was born into a broken family, a missing piece, a place of no security, and no safety.

I heard the stories all my life of what my childhood was like from their perspective. I was given the nickname "Crabby Tabby," I was taunted and criticized; I was accused and abused. No one could heal the pain; no one could fully understand what was missing in my heart; no one could see the scars. I was left in a place of brokenness, forced to be raised in the hands of abusive men who only took advantage of me. I would lay awake in fear, afraid of the darkness that was always so near. I would cry out in anger. Could anyone save me from this place of hurt and betrayal? The hands of men that were supposed to comfort and provide; instead, they hurt me deep inside. Lost, confused, misused, I was raised in the hands of total abuse, yet I was always to blame and grew up deeper and deeper, trying to cover the pain. I never truly knew what peace was, I never knew what life was supposed to be, I only knew my reality, and it caused me to be deeply ashamed. I didn't know how to explain the missing place inside of me. Every one of the "father" figures that married my mother took advantage of me. Beginning at the age of three and until I was a teen, I was abused by three different men.

THE HEART OF THE FATHERLESS

I know the desperate cries and pleas of the heart of the fatherless personally. Night after night, I would lay my head on a pillow filled with tears. I would cry, asking God why, wondering if He was real. I prayed for protection and provision. I remember the pain that gripped my heart. My entire body was filled with fear. The emotional pain was so deep that it hurt my gut physically. I longed for safety. I yearned for protection. I cried, hoping someone would save me. I did not know my true father. My family suffered from extreme poverty. We always had needs that needed to be met. My mother worked long and hard hours to provide, but she was young and hurting inside. She was only sixteen when she first started her family. A child herself doing all she knew to survive, caught in a cycle of abuse with men who promised a fulfilled life. My heart cried to know my father. Who did I belong to? Who did I look like? Who was the one that made me? Why did he reject me? Why did he not love me? Why did he abandon me and leave me in the hands of abuse? Why did we go hungry, and why was I not clothed? Why couldn't we be like every other family? I had no father, and the hands of men I was left in were abusive. My childhood memories are filled with traumatic events. No matter where I turned to for help, I was met with another false hope and hands that didn't protect me. I was violated in every way, and that left me with deep wounds that only God could heal.

CHAPTER 3

The Calling

CHILDLIKE HOPE

When I was a young toddler, I remember it was my first time I tried to run away. I grabbed my little brother and walked out of the front door. I remember telling him, "We gotta get out of here; it's not safe!" I was scared for my life. I wanted to run to a safe place! My little brother was very young, still in diapers, but he followed me. I walked right out onto the busy street, and there were a lot of older people. One lady said, "Where are you going, little one?" as she passed me with her cane, I just looked up and kept going hoping I could be invisible to all these people. I wondered why so many were out on the street; it was extremely busy. The next thing you know, I was sitting in a big leather chair, across from a man with a black suit and a little white square on his collar. I remember feeling so small in that chair as he asked me where I was going and where my home was. I remember telling him I was afraid and ran away. I saw something that morning that frightened me in my mother's skeleton keyhole of her bedroom door, it was what all the bad men had done to me, and I wanted to protect my family. I boldly told the man this, as he kept asking me these questions. I remember I gave him my grandmother's phone number, how I was so smart to know these things, I don't know. But I did. I was assertive and direct. I was tired of the abuse. The next thing I know, I was being handed back to my mother, in the middle of the street that man was threatening my mother, he wasn't showing her any kindness, but he reluctantly released me back into the place I was trying to escape.

These are some of the broken memories I have from my childhood. I was one that may have been angry, broken, and lost, but I had a will, a strong one at that. I always had a deep understanding and knew when things were not right, and I had zero tolerance for people that mistreated others. I still had a strong heart to protect people from what I was facing, even as a young toddler, I was bound to lead and protect people from the evils I had endured. I later realized the man in the black suit and little white square was a priest, and all those people on that busy street were on their way to Sunday morning church. The moment I walked out of the house that day, there was greater protection upon me that I had yet to learn. There was always a force that guided my way even through the pain; I had just not discovered it yet. It took me the unfolding of many hard valleys and places to see what my heart was always longing for from the start was available to me, and His eyes were still upon me, a Father's Love.

Several years later, I was a young school-aged girl, and I remember sitting in a room that was so big. The voices echoed through the empty sanctuary that had just a few people and some kids running around. The sound was different than anything I had heard before. It was a church, a place where people gathered to sing and talk about Jesus. There was a man that would always give us candy. His pockets were full of those delicious caramel delights. I looked forward to going each time, and I remember the joy I had when I went. The abuse seemed to seize for a moment; when we moved in with grandma, and my mom had a new man in her life. There appeared to be a change and a promise for the future. I loved going to church because it gave my heart hope.

Holding that hymnal in my hand, not having any clue what the lines and dots meant, I remember how my heart began to fill with peace and longing as we sang:

"And He walks with me, and He talks with me, and He tells me I am His own, and the joy we share as we tarry there none other has ever known."

I can close my eyes and recall exactly the way I felt. It was a feeling of belonging and hope. All that I ever wanted was written in that song. The feelings of love and security washed over my soul. I longed to walk and talk with Jesus. I desired to belong. I wanted to be protected and directed. My heart yearned for this genuine relationship. Was it true that Jesus knew and loved us?

At night, as a child, I would cry out to Jesus. I prayed all the time. I never really knew if He heard me or if He was truly real, but something deep down inside told me He was, so I kept praying. Every time I heard His name, my heart would leap with hope. I loved to learn about Him. I loved to say His name; I longed to know Him. I would gaze at the stars at night in wonder, and the clouds in the day I would watch with hope. When I was a young child, I would sit in the back of the car, with my head against the window and my eyes fixed on the sky. My heart knew there had to be a God that looked down on us each day. I wondered if it was all true, and if there was a God in heaven who loved me, and when it thundered outside, was that God moving His furniture around? Or when it rained, was He watering His garden of the Earth? My heart searched to know, and I will never forget the days I had a childlike faith.

My grandmother was Catholic; she had crucifixion crosses throughout her house. I remember seeing Jesus on those crosses and just knowing that there was something special about Him. Once, my grandmother took me to her church. She didn't go very often, but I remember it was different from how I knew it. We had a big leather stool at our feet, and at certain times, we would kneel on it and then rise again. I couldn't understand much of what they said, but I was just happy to be with my grandma. She was a true hero to me in so many ways. When I was young, she would swoop me up and give me those great big bear hugs and Eskimo kisses, and I will never forget how I felt completely safe in her arms. She wore necklaces that she never took off, and one of them was a gold cross. I remember how comforting it was to me when she would hug me, and that cross always seemed to catch my eye and bring me comfort that my heart searched to know why.

THE PREACHER

One day at that small church, my family was visiting with the man with delicious caramel delights. I will never forget the time, in the middle of the preacher's sermon, he stopped and came down from the platform and headed straight towards me. I remember the feeling in my stomach of not being sure of what to expect. I am not sure what he was talking about, but I will never forget what he said. *"This young girl has a call of God on her life,"* as he gently held my face in his hands. Something came over me and rested in my heart that day. At that time, it would have been impossible for me to understand and even harder to receive, but that day was a footprint that God was declaring to me that I was His.

HOPE DEFERRED

After several years had passed, our family no longer consistently went to church. I am not sure why we quit going, other than hearing the preacher and his family moved away. We had some life changes; we moved out of my grandmother's house and had our own home. All my mom could afford, and I was proud to have a place to call home. However, the kids at school teased and taunted because it was a mobile home, and everyone knew that we didn't quite belong in the social class of our school. Many of the kids at our school came from medium income families, the working class. However, my family was broken, blended, and afflicted with extreme poverty.

Let me explain; imagine being in a neighborhood filled with beautiful homes with a value of two hundred thousand or more, and at the top of that neighborhood stood our old broken-down mobile home. When I say broken, I mean broken. When it rained outside, the roof leaked so we had to set out pots and pans to collect the rain inside. There were holes in the flooring throughout the whole house. Under the kitchen sink was a hole so great that we had raccoons climb in our kitchen. My grandmother owned the lot that we put our home on; it was all my mom could afford.

I will never forget the day our new home, or should I say, the old home arrived. I was in grade school, and it was an early school day morning; we were all awaiting the school bus at the end of the street with the other kids in our neighborhood. Our home was to be delivered that day. I wasn't expecting the delivery to be at the same time the school bus was picking us up.

However, that is how it happened. We had to wait for the delivery driver to get through the tight corners of our neighborhood circle before we were able to board the bus. There it was, our mobile home, that I was so excited about it until I realized how different we were from rest of the community. When we finally boarded the bus that morning, a lot of the kids laughed at my new home. Most of the kids lived in very nice homes. Seeing a mobile home of that condition move into that neighborhood wasn't something the kids there understood.

I had a tough time with this transition into school and our home, although just up the road from grandma's, all the kids knew where we had lived. I wanted friends and wanted to belong, but now I am bullied daily on the school bus for my poor conditions. I remember running up that large hill when I would get off the school bus, in tears, crying mom, the kids at school don't like me. They tease me that hate me. She tried to comfort me by saying all that means they like you. But I knew that wasn't true at all. I felt tormented every day that I had to go to school. So once again, my heart was shattered in more ways than one. I was proud of my mom and knew she did all she could have done, but the kids at school didn't understand, and my heart was too fragile even to comprehend.

My mother's new husband wasn't the hope she hoped he would become. He couldn't keep a job to help provide and struggled with alcohol dependency. He not only abused my mother physically, and she wore the bruises to prove it with blackened eyes and shattered teeth. In his drunken rage, I remember one day I thought for sure he was going to kill my mother, I shouted and shouted, but nothing I did stopped his anger as he repeatedly rammed my mother's head into our front door. On top of witnessing my mother's severe beatings, this stepdad began to abuse me sexually. Several times a week, while my mother was at work, he would pull me into his room and violate my innocence night after night.

I felt so dirty and ashamed. I had no way to escape this place. I was terrified for my mother's safety, and my heart cried for safety for my brother and sisters. I hated life; I hated that this was happening again. I thought we were on the road to hope, to find out we are just in another chapter of abuse. When I was teased and rejected by my peers, I thought it was because somehow, they could see the dirty smudges of what I lived through night after night. I was so insecure and afraid. I wanted to be free but did not want to bring shame to my mother, who I knew was trying as hard as she could. I felt as though if I told what was happening, it would only depress her worse than she already was.

I had already been abused several times in my young life as young as a toddler. I was only three years old, and I remember a stepdad staring me straight in the eyes, threatening if I told anyone what he did, the devil would come and kill my entire family. I was terrified. When I was about seven or eight, another stepdad's relative that stayed with us at the time would pull me into his room and forced me to watch terrible things, and then he would take advantage of me. One night he came into my room, pulled me out of bed, and attempted to rape me terribly. I remember crying at the pain and how physically violating it was. He reeked of cigarettes and alcohol, and that stench is one I will never forget. Thankfully one day, my mom witnessed him inappropriately touching me and confronted him and forced him to leave. If I remember correctly, a terrible fight broke out, and she endured another beating, but that man finally left our house.

"TABETHA, ARE YOU COMING IN TODAY?"

At the young age of eleven or twelve, I found myself searching the streets for acceptance and protection. I was so angry and hurting very deep inside. Every beacon of hope only flickered for a moment, and then the light seemed to turn dim quickly. I was so lost and confused. I carried a weight of dark secrets to protect my family. I endured the suffering because I didn't want anyone to feel as terrible as I did. After all these times, I somehow thought something had to be wrong with me, and I must have deserved this life I was given. I questioned myself, not knowing who I was and why my birth father did not come to rescue me. Every father-like figure in my life let me down by abandonment or abuse, and I was utterly lost and longed for freedom from all the trauma that I had lived through.

All my life, I felt the stings of rejection and vicious abuse. When I was that small child, holding that hymnal in my hands singing those songs that brought me hope was indeed the only rescue I could have known. But things did not get any better; they only got worse. I felt like my life was a disaster, and no one seemed to come and change my situation. We faced yet again another battle, after battle, after battle. I felt like everywhere I was, there was a battle. In my home, I battled watching my mom being abused physically. At night, I battled a man coming into my room to abuse me. On the school bus, I battled bullying, on the playground being left alone and isolated, with no friends to turn to. Everywhere I turned, I was in a battle. My heart was sick because the hope of peace, love, and security wasn't what I knew. I knew the calamity of abuse. I ran to find hope in ways that could take away the pain.

One Sunday morning, I was walking down the street alone, and I passed by that little church my family used to visit years ago when there was a flicker of hope. As I walked by, the new pastor who knew my family stood in the doorway and asked, "Tabetha, are you coming in today?" as he held open the doors.

I walked by with my head, hung down in complete shame, and said, "No, not today." You see, I was beginning to move in a different direction. I didn't trust anyone or anything. The only thing that brought me comfort was to be with people who understood me. Who I was accepted by, and who I could relate to. No one else listened to me or cared enough to stop what was going on. I learned early in life that you could not trust anyone, and you had to fear everything. I had to find safety in being the outcast because normal life did not receive me. I adventured onto a road that would.

Later in my life, I was able to look back on that very day and see a significant footprint of the Father's love reaching out to me on the road to rebellion. He was still calling me His very own and beckoning me to come into the only place I would find true safely, in His arms of love. But it took many more encoun-ters to reach my heart, and you will see as we journey through the next chapters in this story of a faithful Father's love.

CHAPTER 4

The Road to Rebellion

CYCLE OF ABUSE

Abuse is a terrible cycle to live in; if you have ever experienced any form of it, you know how hard it can be to overcome the severe mental anguish, emotional scars, and deep imprints it leaves in your soul. You cannot undo what has been done; no matter how hard you try; you cannot clean what has been damaged. Your innocence is stolen. You have been exposed to the horrendous acts of sin and violated in every way. It is a cycle; a cycle is something that continues. It is hard to escape and even harder to overcome, especially without knowing the only one that holds the real power to restore the human heart.

A cycle of abuse leads you into a place of constant anxiety, deep depression, and severe post-traumatic stress. Your days are filled with unbearable feelings, with fear on every side. You long to trust and have relationships but are afraid to open up and let anyone inside. You want to be healed but are so scared to uncover your wounds, hoping not to be taken advantage of, or worse, fear being labeled and rejected as scared. If you share what has been done, will people see you as a product of abuse and no longer accept you? Your sleep is disrupted, you can't find real rest. Anxious thoughts fill your mind; anger and hatred of yourself afflict your soul. Hopelessness and loneliness are all you know.

WRONG ROAD

With no one realizing the suffering I was living in; school became challenging for me. Going to school made it worse because the rejection I faced only highlighted feelings marked by the abuse. I carried a great weight of shame. I would find myself changing in the bathroom stalls in the locker rooms. My body was an enemy to me, and I was embarrassed by it. I was afraid of the taunting and teasing and the terrible names they called me. They would make fun of my name and call me "Flabatha." I did not have nice clothes. I would wear the same things day after day. I probably didn't smell very good and don't remember having excellent hygiene. I never knew how to fix my hair or dress nicely.

Ever since I could remember, I wanted to look like a boy instead of a girl. I asked for short haircuts and wore baggy clothes. I was hiding my identity as a girl because of the pain it caused me. But what hurt worse was not when they made fun of me, but when my brother and sister were teased. I always felt a deep conviction to protect my family; maybe it was because of the lies I was told when I was three that it was my duty to protect them against the devil by keeping those secrets. I am not sure, but I remember when they hurt, it hurt me. Once my little brother wet his pants, we had this terrible stepdad that lifted him by his neck and threw him across the room. I stood there shaking right next to the phone and wanted to call 911 but feared the unknown. My brother's head slammed into the coffee table, and he almost caught his eye.

The doctor said a millimeter closer, and he would have been blind. My little brother had issues and was bullied along with me; my older sister always silently bared it and carried on. I still don't know how she did it, but she went everyday clear until twelfth grade. It was torture to me, and I could not endure it any longer.

Living in mental anguish as I did, it did not take long to find a way to numb the pain. I refused to go to school; I would find every way to escape going to that place. I would jump out of my window and hide in the woods; I hated being humiliated and teased every day. I became truant and was on a path of destructive troubles. I eventually found a group of friends like me, and we went down the wrong path together, smoking marijuana and partying at a very young age. I found a way to manage the pain, friends that accepted me, and the drugs that numbed me and gave us all a way of escape.

Reckless partying, and year after year, it only got worse. The high was never enough, and it never took away the deep scars, but we all found a new way of living, a place to belong. Smoking pot wasn't enough; we kept turning to stronger things. I could tell you story after story of the times and troubles and the places drug addiction took me; it was no good place to be. Eventually, you don't recognize yourself anymore. You find yourself doing whatever it takes to get high and score another bag. If you had the drugs, you had friends. Instead of homework and sports, your school nights turned into looking for another way to get high. We were so desperate that a friend's brother told us about huffing; it was a cheap way to get high. We were desperate, and the things we did were reckless and very dangerous.

The partying lifestyle led me to hopeless places; it is only God's grace that I am alive. I eventually took more than just pain pills and pot but started doing cocaine and heroin as it swept through my town and became available to me. I found myself in full-blown crack houses, strung out on drugs with people I didn't even know. One time, I went out with people I barely knew, and after a full night of smoking crack, I had to walk up a huge snowy hill to get home. I was up all night until the next daybreak, smoking drugs, and I was extremely strung out. My body was so weak and sick that I couldn't hold my bladder, so I lost control right there in the middle of the street. The friends I was with didn't make sure I was safe; they left me off in that street alone that day; I wasn't even eighteen years old. I was just a kid lost in a terrible world.

Heroin is still an epidemic in my hometown; each year, you hear of another person who lost their lives by overdose. I know people I have gone to school with that have lost their lives, too young even to imagine. A whole life is gone, just like that as a vapor in the wind. Here today and gone tomorrow. They didn't have a real chance to live. I know the addictions they had cost them everything. My heart is gripped with grief over those that didn't overcome it. I know my testimony of overcoming can hold the keys of hope to those still held by drug abuse and the chains of addiction. I long to share it with everyone that will hear, hoping they receive and become entirely free and fully restored to the life of Christ we all have been given. For the last fourteen years, I have fought long and hard to testify of the truth of Jesus because I know the power of His name can change someone's life like mine and allow them to be truly free.

Heroin addiction was my ultimate low. I could not believe who I had become and failed to realize at the time the high it could have nearly cost me my life. When you are doing it, you don't think it will happen to you. You do not realize the abuse you are putting your body through. Remember the cycle of abuse I talked about? The abuse continues, but now you are the one that is abusing yourself; you turn to drug abuse and destroy your body, inflicting false relief that is only slowly and sometimes suddenly killing you.

I will share one story about heroin use because I want you to see the grace of God in my life. Years after, God healed me from my difficult past. I was in a church meeting, and a very popular preacher was ministering. We were all at the altar worshiping, and he stopped for a moment and asked us all to reflect and ask the Lord to reveal a time in our lives that the grace of God kept us. I was a young Christian, very excited about the truth and love I found in Jesus. I could not wait, so I closed my eyes, fully expecting to hear from the Lord, and saw like a movie a vision of this day in my life that I had forgotten all about.

On this day, I saw each detail very clear. I could see the green chair I sat in my mattress on the floor, the curtain that hung in my doorway as my door. I had a blue box on my dresser that I kept my drugs in. I had a bag of heroin, and I was alone and decided to use the drugs. I never used heroin alone before, so I never actually prepared it myself. I had a needle and thought I might as well shoot it. I never did that before. I usually would snort the drugs. This day was different, and I am not sure why. I do remember, particularly, my heart was extra heavy, and I felt alone. I cooked the drugs in a spoon, not sure how to use it. I just did what I saw others do. I put the drug in the needle and then injected it into my vein. As this memory-filled my heart, I saw something that I did not see before. Jesus was standing right behind me as I sat in that green chair. I saw Jesus in the room with me!

As tears flooded my eyes, I realized that was the day I would have died. The Lord revealed He was with me, keeping me alive! After I took those drugs that day, I was higher than I had ever been before. I became extremely sick and felt the room spin around me. I laid on that mattress for the next several days, unable to eat or drink; my body could not keep anything down. I was unable to sleep, my body was tired, but my mind was wide awake. I ached from head to toe. Nothing I did stopped the deep pain in my body. I threw up for days; my little sister walked past me in the bathroom one day and said, "Tabby, are you alright?" As my head was buried in the toilet. She was the only one to notice me that I nearly lost my life during those several days. I told her, "Ya Val, I am alright," and dismissed her. I did not want to worry her, but you could see the concern in her eyes. She knew I was not alright. After this encounter with the Lord, I learned even more; I was not okay. I was on the brink of losing my life. Had it not been for His love, I would have died. Even today, my heart is gripped with the truth that I am alive only by His grace. I will never forget the day I saw Jesus standing with me, in the deepest darkest moment of my life. I try to live every day in this truth, so I do not take for granted the life I have been given. I hope to reach people with the same love He reached me with, to share the faithful love of a Father. God, I pray that they will see your grace is enough for us to live.

FALSE LOVE AND SECURITY

Going back to the beginning, what is it we all long for? A father's love, a place of acceptance and security. All the decisions I made to bring comfort to my heart was because I was searching for love in all the wrong places. The drugs gave me a place of escape, and my friends made me feel like I was not alone. I had a connection with my friends that no one else could give me. Men all betrayed me; they did nothing but harm. I did not trust any of them; I hide my identity as a girl behind ponytails and baggy clothes. I did not fit in. I knew nothing about makeup and how to be feminine. I felt ugly and despised by the boys, especially those on the bus that would tease me. I was utterly lost looking for love in all the wrong places.

I found comfort, but it was not healthy or real. It was out of false love and security. I had a close friend that struggled to, and she, however, portrayed to care for me deeply; she made me feel special and loved. She was my very best friend, the only person I have ever trusted. I told her everything that I had gone through; we were so close and never apart. Our friendship turned into something more, and we found comfort in one another in a relationship that wasn't true or pure. It was just another way to numb the pain.

This relationship gave me security. I had someone I could trust and share my deepest emotions with. That was all I longed for, was someone to know and love me, that understood me, who accepted me. Who embraced me, stood with me, and saw me as something worth to love. I trusted her because she was not a man. Men wanted to use me for my body, but she connected with me emotionally. I did not feel threatened by her because the connection was greater than physical. So, I opened my life up to having a sexual relationship with her. I thought it was how I was created. I thought it was the only way for me to experience true love and security. Men terrified me. Ever since I was a small child, I saw them as a predator, not a companion, a perpetrator not a protector. They all wanted one thing, my body. But my friend didn't afflict that harm. She "loved" me for me; she desired a relationship with me for who I was. That gave me so much security and created a very codependent relationship. My life became all about this one relationship. I would have given anything for this love because it was what I thought I was searching for all along.

I don't doubt that we shared a real love for one another. It was very real to us, but it does not mean it was healthy and right. I found out later in life what "true love" is and who it comes from. I can assure you what we experienced was as real as it seemed, but it was not a love that completes, that heals, that mends, and truly satisfies the deep longings of our soul. Our love for one another was out of brokenness, emotional dependence, it was tainted love. Our love for each other didn't satisfy or heal; it was never enough. We had to keep returning to it like a drug. We created a dependence on it like we did for everything. The love I eventually found brought true freedom to my soul and set all things right. We were all trying to find our way the best way we knew how. But once you fully understand the truth, it will set you free! I still love all the people that have been in my life, but the love I have now is different from what I knew before. It is the agape love of God, and this love is a love we can all become dependent on! His love heals and mends and restores our weary souls.

CHAPTER 5

The Rescue

The love I grew so dependent on had eventually let me down. My friend had left, and my world was upside down. I spent most of my days working at a pizza shop and getting high alone. Sure, I had friends, but none like the one I loved. My heart was broken, and the hope I had was gone. My assurance of belonging was ripped away. I quit using heavy drugs for the most part and started to soul search. I got a hold of a CD that I believe God used to reach me. One song was called, "God Blessed the Broken Road," these songs had so much power in them; they spoke to my soul about true love. Even though I have not experienced it yet, I was changing, and God used these songs to soften my broken heart.

My mother was praying for me that God would send someone into my life to help me. She knew I was addicted to this relationship that was gone; she knew I was doing drugs and afflicting self-harm. She knew but could not reach me. She knew God had to send someone that would love me back to life. At that time, my mother had a Godsend; the Lord had given my mother a new husband that took her to church and gave her the security she needed to mend. He was a blessing for her, but for me, I needed something more.

Men had done nothing but hurt me all my life, so I did not want a husband or anything to do with any men ever. I never saw myself in any other kind of lifestyle than the one I was living. But my heart was growing to change, and there was one man that I had said I would marry several years ago.

My mother can retell the day I went to a relative's house to begin guitar lessons, and while I was there, a friend of the relative was also visiting. I remember the first time I saw him; I instantly knew there was something different about him. I came home that day and said, "Mom, I met the only man I will ever marry today." To this day, I still have no other explanation for what I said, outside of it being God-ordained. Nothing special had taken place. I remember him sitting in the chair, talking to those that were there. I don't know if he even recognized me or not. I didn't have any desire or burning in my heart, those words just came straight out of my mouth, and I had not taken any thought to it.

With my mother's prayers, my lonely despair, and these songs that sang my heart's desire's, everything was about to change because God was working out everything in His perfect way. My life was on the verge of drastically changing when the only man I said I would ever marry several years ago came to the house to visit the family. He was the answer God was sending to change my life.

FALLING IN LOVE

There was something so different about David; I had peace with him. He never made me feel afraid; I knew he was genuine. It was as if I trusted him from the beginning. He took care of me like no one had. On our very first date together, he took me out to eat. I never experienced anyone taking me on a proper date and treating me with such dignity. I was shy with him a lot of the times, but I didn't hold back from telling him all my stories. I think he was shocked by the life I lived, but he didn't judge me or label me for the things I did. He didn't seem to be afraid of the paths I had taken. More than anything, I think he wanted to love me and take care of me. He was a professional driver at the time and would go on the road for weeks at a time. I knew I was in love when he would leave, and I would go into the bathroom at work and cry. David brought my life hope; I felt safe with him; I felt like I could have a better life. But when he would go over the road, I was too broken to stand alone. I needed someone to carry me through each day, and David was that to me.

MARRYING YOUNG

I remember riding up the long hills; we were headed to a place that David had prepared to take me. Everything was an adventure with David. We had just been dating for a few short months, but we both had fallen in love. He was different from anyone I had ever known. His love gave me hope. David was quiet, calm, and reserved. In David's arms, I truly felt safe. He loved to hear my stories, and I loved to listen to his dreams. He saw something in me that I did not even see. David had so many plans for the future; I never heard anyone talk like him; he wanted to travel the world, build companies, raise a family, and seize every opportunity. He saw the world differently from me, and I admired that.

Driving through the mountains, he parked the truck and had me follow him. The sun had just set, and we are standing in the middle of a snowy field. He told me how beautiful this place was and how he planned to be here before nightfall. But right there, David got on his knee and asked me to marry him; he vowed to want to spend the rest of his life with me.

I remember feeling shaky; I couldn't believe that anyone would ever want to marry me. Marriage wasn't even a thought to me at eighteen years old; I stood there, not sure what this all really meant, but I knew my answer was yes. I couldn't imagine my life without the only one I could trust enough to love. I didn't understand marriage, family, and or what it meant to build a life together. I never even envisioned myself getting married! But years ago, I did say he would be the only man I would marry. I don't think my broken young heart understood the journey that had just begun, but I was willing to go forward unprepared, but with a willing heart to go. I trusted this man with my life, and I vowed to be his wife. I pushed away every doubt and insecurity and hoped that this would be the start of a better life.

Within a few short months of the proposal, we made the marriage official; my family arranged a small gathering with our immediate families and the preacher's family. It was a nice setting, an elegant dinner spread, a beautiful wedding cake, and flowers, which my family provided. I was so naive about being womanly. I didn't even own a dress. Or have the knowledge to go and buy that special wedding gown. I was a simple girl who never knew how to be ladylike. I worked at a pizza shop and spent most of my money on marijuana. Caring for myself wasn't a priority. I had no self-confidence or self-esteem. As we stood before the preacher with David in a tie and me in a simple summer dress, the preacher read the vows, it was my turn to place the ring on David's finger, and as I did, I was shaky and dropped it to the ground. I was so embarrassed! I already felt completely unprepared; I hurried to pick up the ring, as I did the preacher said, "Tabetha, just like in life, you will drop this, but you will pick it right back up." I picked the ring back up and placed it on his finger. I didn't realize the importance of what the preacher said until later in my life, but looking back, I can see it was the Lord encouraging me every step of the way that everything was going to be alright.

The preacher wrote our marriage vows, and it highlights:

"As we gather at this time to unite this couple, David, and Tabetha in Holy Matrimony, let us Pray.

As we can in-vision in our minds on a mountain side there is a spring of water or a beginning. On the other side of the mountain is another spring of water or a beginning and as two streams of water flow down each side of the mountain, they come together or they meet, then they are together for a period of time. This represents David and Tabetha, now they have met, and their relationship grows stronger. They are flowing in the river of life together. You see as a river flows along, many things are built around the rivers there are villages, towns, resorts, business establishments, mills, and factories and many many things as your life as of today, the river of life is bringing many new phases into your lives. You now have father and mother laws, sister and brother in laws, new aunts and uncles, new cousins, already your lives on this river is expanding, then there are children, grandchildren, and great grandchildren, then the river flows on into the ocean or a sea of eternity. In so many words- from here to eternity. "

Everything happened so fast. One day I am alone in my room, singing songs about true love. The next I am getting married in a simple summer dress to the man I said would be the only man I would marry several years ago. It is indescribable how this story unfolds, but all I can say it was the hand of God that mended the pieces that we share today. The pastor that married David and I was the same pastor that stood in the doorway of the church and called out, *"Tabetha, are you coming in today?"*

My life was changing drastically and at an expedited rate. I was only a few short months out of heroin addiction, and I have this man of great integrity and purpose, wanting to spend the rest of his life with me? He was a marine, a soldier, an entrepreneur, a man of dreams. He has already accomplished so much in his early twenties, and I am nothing more than a recovering drug addict who is troubled in most people's eyes. But not David, he saw in me, more than I could ever see, he saw a future and a hope, and he had no motive outside of loving me and wanting to spend the rest of his life with me.

BECOMING A MOM

I was eighteen years old, married, and expecting our first son. It's hard to imagine that I had journeyed through all those times in my short young life. I was still recovering from the trauma of my past and trying to adjust to my new life. I quit smoking cigarettes and marijuana to keep my body clean for the protection of our son. It was the first time in my life I could remember being completely sober-minded. I had a life dependent upon me, so I tried my hardest to become better than what I was.

I remember the terrible anxiety I had about becoming a mother, the fears, worries, and hopes that I would be able to be a good mom, and the dread and worry that I would not be. I felt inadequate in every way, I was just as lost as anyone could be, and now I need to lead the way. I knew very little about family; I knew even less about being a wife or a mom.

I spent the entire nine months trying to prepare for Jacob the best I knew how. I watched the dreaded baby stories on labor and delivery daily! That scared me out of my mind! I feared having a c-section and hoped to have a safe and normal delivery. I ate ice cream every single day. I knew nothing about moderation and healthy lifestyles. So, I splurged on food when pregnant and gained nearly eighty pounds! I figured it was way better than smoking and doing drugs. I couldn't bear to think of risking Jacob's health over my habits. We had

Jacob's nursery all prepared in our home that David was renovating for us. David was busy working and remodeling to prepare a home for our new family.

The day came that I went into labor for the very first time. It was complicated, I was in labor all day and night with no progression. I had severe back labor. I refused medications because I wanted to do it naturally for my son. But I eventually had to have the epidural because the pain was unbearable. When I finally was able to push, they rushed me into the operating room for a c-section. Jacob's heart rate would drop every time I went to push. He was in distress, and the labor and delivery stories were now happening to us!

Thank God we had a successful c-section. I remember holding Jacob in my arms for the very first time; it was an overwhelming love. I laid in my hospital bed flat on my back as they wheeled me out of the operation room. I remember the pain; it was like a burning fire as the medicine wore off. But this life in my hands and my heart was the most beautiful beginning to a new start. Excitement and joy-filled our hearts when we brought Jacob to our home. We have become our very own family.

CYCLES OF ANGER & PAIN

If you don't deal with the root cause of why we do the things we do, we can't possibly stop the cycles in our life from taking place. This is exactly where I was, I was a new mom who stayed clean during pregnancy, and I was a new wife trying to adapt to this life that I felt entirely unprepared for. I decided to go back to work right after Jacob was born. I bought a pack of cigarettes on my way home from the hospital; now that I could freely smoke without affecting him, I did. My life changed, but I still didn't know how to handle it all. It was easier for me to go to work than to face the fears of being a new mom. I had such anxiety that I could not function. I would double, triple, quadruple check everything all the time. At night I could not rest well at all; I would wake up regularly to check on Jacob and watch to make sure he was breathing properly. I was on edge about all the things the hospital told me to prevent and wanted to triple check. One night, I remember I fell asleep and woke up in a sheer panic, that I had lost all my children. I yelled out to my husband, where are our children and rattled off name after name; for some reason, I thought we had four children instead of one. David calmly said Jacob is asleep in his crib. I demanded to know where the others were; he kept repeating Jacob is in his crib asleep. I finally realized and went back to bed.

I had severe post-traumatic stress and was afflicted with anxiety; the scars of my past trauma remained. I never fully recovered from my past that was not all that long ago. I still carried a heavy burden in my soul. I was afraid all the time and became overwhelmed and wanted to protect my son, that it would be hard for me to sleep without worrying about his wellbeing and safety. No one could have prepared me for the challenges and significant life changes of becoming a mom for the very first time.

In general, this can be a hard transition for any new mom, with the depression that can accompany it. But with me, and already battling and self-medicating so much, this wasn't easy to overcome. The last thing I wanted was not to provide or protect my son, so I did the best I knew how to do. I felt like I was in survival mode all the time, instead of enjoying becoming a new mom. Don't get me wrong, I loved my son with all my heart, but I was so filled with fear; it made it impossible to rest. I was afraid I would fail my son as his mom. That is why I found comfort in working and doing what I was used to. I was extremely insecure and felt completely unprepared to be his mom. Maybe that is how my dad saw me, and he thought it was better to fail me not to be there, than to fail me being there.

All my life, I smoked marijuana to cope with anxiety and post-traumatic stress. When I was pregnant with Jacob, I did not. After Jacob was born, I tried to stay free of it. The anger I had was because I was so afraid all the time. All I ever knew was trauma, so I was always waiting for the next bad thing to take place. Not that I wanted it to. But the cycle would always come back again. This is what I learned since I was a child, and although I am a married woman and a mother in many ways, I was still a child. I never had the opportunity to learn how to live or healthily cope with life. I only knew what I knew. I desperately wanted change but didn't know how to overcome the anxiety. I was angry at how I felt and how I could not overcome the fear that controlled my life. It was constant stress, a terrible state I was in.

Eventually, things started getting complicated at home. Dave and I were at each other all the time, we both were doing our best, but it was difficult for everyone. We both loved each other deeply, and our child unconditionally, but the cycle of anger and pain was still in my soul. I was always anxious and afraid, and I tried to handle it the best way I knew how. Old friends started coming around, and they were shocked that I was married and had a son. They were the only comfort I knew growing up. I was having a difficult time transitioning into a new life without self-medicating. When the friends came around, it was like an old way of coping came back to me and life's temptation got the best of me. Little at a time, I started to return to the party lifestyle and all the while leaving David to care for our son.

This all took place during our first two years of marriage. Although I loved my husband and son, I didn't feel like I could manage this life, I was too drawn to the old ways, and I hated what I was becoming. I was becoming a mom who wasn't home; I was becoming a wife that wasn't faithful; I was doing the things I longed not to do. I didn't want to act this way, I just wanted a normal life, and now that I had the opportunity to do normal as best as I could, the pain and insecurities of my past were robbing me of my future. I hated myself for what I could not control. I was doing the things I did not want to do and could not do what I wanted to. I mistreated Dave, and I wanted him to leave me. I wanted him to let me go, so he did not have to deal with this anymore. I would beg him to leave me, but he would not. He had every reason to give up, and I am sure at times he wanted to, but he did not.

I could not understand how someone could love me enough to stay with me; after everything I had done, how could he still love me, how could he still see the hope in me when I saw none. I could not understand how to handle the issues of life. When something was hard for me, I tended to run. I ran away my whole life, jumped out of my window instead of going to school, quit jobs instead of finishing, started projects but never saw them through until the end; the deep wounds and insecurities drove me never to think I would be good enough to finish anything. I begged David to leave me as everyone else did, I hated what I was becoming, and it was easier for me to quit and run than stay and endure and overcome. But David would not leave me; although I am sure he struggled at times, he committed to me, and he was faithful to fulfill his word to me.

DIVINE INTERVENTION

David and I were having troubles on every side, and I was endlessly searching for ways to run and hide. I had fallen into some old patterns with old friends; I spent most of my days working and going out at night. I was humiliated at what I had become. I didn't know how to be a wife or a mom.

One afternoon, David got a call that his grandma would be passing away very soon and she may not have much more time with us. David loved his grandmother with all of his heart; she was his absolute favorite; he had an extraordinary bond with her. Grandma was diagnosed with dementia several years ago. I remember meeting her. She would sing songs in a different language and always wore a great big smile; she was the most joyful person I have ever met.

Every time we visited, it was hard on David because she never recognized him as her grandson. He always would say he wished I could have met her before all of this. Dementia robbed grandma of all her memories, all except for being a schoolteacher and never getting sick. David pleaded with me to go with him to visit grandma;

he wanted to say his final goodbyes. I knew he needed me to go, I, however, remember feeling uncomfortable and inadequate with going to this kind of visit, but I pressed through and went anyway.

When we got to grandma's room, the lights were lowered dim. David's parents were both in the room, and grandma laid happily in her bed. David, with tears filling his eyes, walked softly over to her bedside. Grandma turned her face towards him and said, "I can see the chariots of fire ready to take me home. I am ready to go; they are here for me." David was so sorrowful; I remember him pouring out his heart, telling grandma how much he loved her. I shyly stood behind him, not exactly sure what to do.

As he held her hand, she started to speak the oracles of God; she told David very specific things in our lives that were a mess, and how to not worry God's hand was on us, and it was all going to be okay. She spoke from a place of great knowledge, knowing specific details to our struggles as in our finances and our personal matters. David's parents, who were in the room, could not understand what she was saying. It was like their understanding had been completely closed to hear. They murmured on the other side of the room, "What is she saying? We don't understand."

David knew it was God speaking directly to him, and he received every word. He urged me to come near her and hold grandma's hand. I, however, was stricken with fear and could not bring myself to do that. I was so afraid. Grandma then said, "You can understand why she is afraid; it is okay; don't force her; she will be okay." When she spoke with such great compassion and understanding, I inched my way a bit closer, I still could not bring myself to her hand, but I came close to her side. She then turned to me and gently told me to be honest and don't forget the letter. My heart struck within me because I was not being honest with David; I was keeping many things from him. With these words from grandma, I somehow thought it could all be okay if I could get the courage to be honest. I timidly turned towards the door because my heart could not bear any more. Everything in me felt like it was shaking. As I walked away, grandma turned towards me and said, "I will not forget you, girl, I will not forget you." Grandma's aged eyes were covered in cataracts, and I was on the other side of this dim lightroom, trying to walk away quietly. She turned and looked straight at me, with perfect clarity, knowing where I stood and would not let me leave without knowing that I was loved and known by her. What is so significant was in all my fear and sin, the hand of God still declared that I was His. Because it was not Grandma that was speaking, it was the one true living God, and He said He would not forget me. She then told David, "Be patient and hang in there, you are going to lead her to Calvary, and everything is going to be alright."

That night we drove home, I don't remember much of what we said, but I remember how I felt; David said I was rattled and afraid, confused, and asked him what just happened there. He said I was flipping out in more ways than not because I did not understand it was the spirit of the sovereign Lord, bringing us a message of hope. I could not understand how she knew all she did, and it was beyond my ability to know all that had taken place in the room that day. All my life, I cried out to know Jesus, but I never realized Calvary was the place I would need to go. I did not know what Calvary even meant, and I didn't know God knew all there was to know about the exact details of our lives and could speak through people like you and me. *This was another miraculous footprint in my journey; this time, I was on my way to Calvary.*

CHAPTER 6

The Ransom

GOING TO MY FATHER'S HOUSE

Some time had passed since we had visited grandma, she ended up staying with us a little longer. She lived a long life of a hundred years. She was a beacon of light and changed many lives by her faithful prayers and steadfast hope in Jesus. It was after we visited Grandma, David had a change in his heart too. He grew up in the church and knew he needed to raise our son in the house of the Lord. I was still naive to understand any of these things. But David insisted we needed to go. That Sunday morning, he urged me to get ready. It would be our first time going to church as a family. I slammed my bedroom door, shouted terrible words, argued, and complained, I made excuses about not wanting to be late. However, David was unmovable in his stand and insisted we go. I realize now; it wasn't me that was angry; it was the enemy of my soul that fought against the plan God had already set out for me on the road to Calvary.

When I walked into the church, it was unlike any place I have ever seen; it was different, people were waving flags and worshiping everywhere; instead of pews, the room was filled with chairs. I still remember the doorkeeper, the usher with a flag in her hand. I remember her friendly face and the love in her heart. I remember thinking this is something I never felt before; there was real peace here. I feared it and almost wanted to run out the door. I forced myself to stay, to sit down, and resisted every urge to leave. I listened to the sermon and felt like he was preaching right to me. I could not understand how the words he preached read my heart so clearly. I knew it was different, and it caught my attention.

The people of the church all welcomed us with love. It did not take long to develop relationships with them. We continued to go, and each time I felt that same way as the preacher knew me and what I was going through. A new friend of mine asked me if I would come to a women's conference that they were having soon. I was so new to church functions, and I remember asking what a women's conference was? She explained that it was just like church, only with women, and it would be an all-day event. I accepted the invitation to go, and she gave me a flyer to remind me of the date.

BRIDGING THE GAP WITH LOVE

It was a Saturday afternoon, and I was getting ready to do what I would typically do, go out with my friends. I was sitting in my room, getting prepared for my night. I had no good plans and still wasn't fully walking in the light. My husband walked in and gently asked me what my plans were, seeing that I was preparing to leave. I told him I was going out with some friends, and he reminded me of the conference that I had committed to. I forgot that today was the day, so I decided to blow it off and continue with my plans anyway. He again reminded me, "Didn't you say that you would go?" I replied, "Yes, I did." David said, "Tabby, you never keep your word; you should try to commit to what you said you would do."

I knew David was right. Usually, I would argue to get my way. But I liked the church and my new friends, and I knew it was the right thing to do, so I went. I walked in wearing my Rolling Stones t-shirt, ripped up blue jeans, and biker boots. I looked around, and the room was filled with nicely dressed ladies. I looked like I was going to a rock and roll concert, and they well were clothed in their Sunday best. I am pretty sure I was a little late but made my effort to keep my word. I found my new friend. She welcomed me and helped me find a place to sit.

The worship service began, and the people did exactly like my friend said they would. Everyone began to worship like on a Sunday morning, but tonight was different. Something came over me; I couldn't keep my heart from weeping in sorrow. The music was so heavenly; it touched me so deeply. It felt alive. Every sound and word moved me. As I sat in my seat, and I could not stop crying, I felt the weight of all my life resting on my shoulders. I felt the heaviness of my soul.

I saw a woman over to my left, with her hands raised high as she danced with all her might. I remember looking over, and the question arose in my heart, "How can she be so free to dance like that?" I didn't speak what I felt, I wasn't gazing at her, these were the quiet petitions of my heart that only God could hear. I could see there was real freedom in her, and it moved me to know why. My heart felt like a billion tons, it was so heavy, and I wanted to know the freedom she did.

THE ENCOUNTER

A precious lady tapped me on my shoulder and spoke softly in my ear, "Honey, God wants me to tell you he wants you free to dance." I jumped to my feet and wanted to run straight to the door. But I searched for my friend. I was crying so hard words cannot even explain. It was like a tidal wave of emotions inside of me, and it was all coming out. I could not run and hide anymore.

I found my friend and explained what just happened; someone told me that God had a message for me. I still didn't realize at the time that yes; God speaks to and through his people. She calmed me down and told me it was expected and encouraged me to sit back down and rest in that.

So, I forced myself to sit back down and try to understand what was happening and why I felt the way I did. I decided to ask God if he was really real. I sat in my seat, and in my heart, I cried out. I can still hear my voice echo within me, asking God to reveal Himself to me. In my heart, with my eyes closed tightly, I cried out, "God, if you are truly real, I will serve you for the rest of my life, but I need to know you are real, so I am asking you to prove yourself to me right now and come down from heaven and wrap your arms around me, and just give me a hug."

I thought I was asking God a hard thing, but it was what I needed from Him. I needed that hug, I needed to see, I needed to know, and longed for that assurance of love and acceptance. I wanted someone to trust, I longed for what was right, I wanted to have this peace that I saw, this joy, this freedom, but I had to know it was something I could truly trust and that I could build my life upon. I had put my life in the arms of false love long enough, and everyone had let me down. I couldn't bear to be taken advantage of anymore. My heart wanted to know, and the only way I could see is if He loved me enough to come down from heaven and hug me.

At the very moment, with no delay, a beautiful woman of God came and sat down right next to me and wrapped her arms around me, and gave me the greatest hug I would ever receive. She didn't ask me. She just swooped me up in the arms of pure love. I laid my head on her chest, and rivers of tears streamed from my eyes. I sobbed and sobbed because I finally knew it was all true. God is alive! He is true! He loves me enough to hug me at my heart's cry. I had no more questions or wondering in my soul. I belonged, and I knew today I was ransomed in His arms of love and truth.

I knew in my heart that He is love. I could feel it all over me; the heaviness of my soul was beginning to subside. I felt protected, and I felt alive. I knew He was all I would ever need. This beautiful lady helped me to my feet, as I could barely walk, but I knew I needed to do my part. I had to respond to this love, and I went to the front of the room, to the place they called the altar.

ARE YOU WILLING TO FORGIVE?

As we got to the altar, there was a man. I never met this man at church before; he was there with a group that I didn't recognize. I remember feeling surprised because this was a women's conference. He looked at me and asked me what he could do for me; I believe he asked how he could pray for me. I could barely say a single word because I still could not quite sobbing, and I honestly did not know. My heart was under great conviction, as a powerful love seemed to blanket over my soul.

He asked me to give him a moment, and when he returned, he asked me one question, "Are you willing to forgive me on behalf of all the men that have hurt you in your life?" My heart shook with awe. How could he know what had happened to me? How could he know that it was men that have betrayed and hurt me? I knew instantly this was a true God that knew me intimately, every pain, and every sorrow. I realized just as Jesus had died for my sins; He died for those who have sinned against me. I realized we were all hurt and needed His love and forgiveness.

I didn't hesitate; I didn't have to think about it; I wanted all this weight gone, I wanted to move on, I wanted to forgive. I said, "Yes." At that moment, I entered into the most life-giving truth in my life. I was baptized into a new life by the power of the almighty Holy Spirit. The moment I chose to release all of those that had betrayed and hurt me in my young life was the key that set me free and brought true liberty.

I explain it to people in the only way I can describe. I experienced true deliverance that day. The preacher held me by the face, like that day, I was a small child in the sanctuary, and stared me straight in my eyes, and called out the powers of the enemy. I could feel one by one; those powers leave my body. He called out anxiety, depression, witchcraft, oppression, every lie that held me captive. It was like a vacuum cleaner of my soul, and the powers left through my eyes. I didn't realize the enemy found a way in my life through all the things I was exposed to and did to cover the pain. I was under demonic oppression, and his entry was through the unresolved trauma and pain of my soul.

The power of God was so strong that I could not stand. My entire body moved across the floor at every call. I was submerged into the presence of pure love and overcoming power. I was wholly light and free. I fell out under the power of the one true living God and cried out in pure joy because the woman I was, was no more! Everything in me changed that very moment. I shouted, "Hallelujah! Hallelujah! Hallelujah!" True lasting love, joy, and peace-filled my soul! I have been born again.

I was filled with a new life, and all it took was my willingness to let go, believe, and receive all Jesus had for me. For the first time in my life, I was completely clean. No one can undo the stains of abuse. Only the blood and power of Jesus could cleanse me. The Lord did not stop there. He had me in His hands. I was surrounded by the most amazing people who knew the heart and voice of our Lord. They gathered around me as I laid on the floor, under this cloud of glory that restored my soul. They continued to pray and speak life. They prophesied and spoke directly to my life in powerful words of knowledge.

This group of people knew nothing about me. They were visitors, as I was. As they prayed, they spoke and released words of truth and purpose from my Father. They said that my past paths would not be the paths of my future, that God was naming my path success, and everything was going to be made new. That everything in my life that the enemy had used to harm me, God was going to turn it around for good and keep it good. They spoke that my shoes were changing, and I no longer was to wear those heavy boots but freely dance before the Lord. They prophesied that my husband and I were a ministry team together that the Lord would use to counsel and guide others. He spoke that I felt like an inadequate mother, but I wasn't because the Lord was going to teach me how to be a parent, and my children were going to grow up and say they had the coolest mom, and I would have a great relationship with my kids. He advised me not to listen to others that were putting me down on my parenting. The Lord also instructed me to not compare myself to other people and how they parent, but to lean on the Lord because I would be different and successful. At that time, I had many people trying to critique me, and it was very difficult, especially with already feeling inadequate. It was a tremendous word of hope that my kids would have extraordinary lives from the Lord. Still, I receive criticism and critique from many well-meaning people about my parenting and many compliments until this day. All three of my children are fantastic; they love the Lord with all their hearts, they love people unconditionally, they love their family, and they are filled with the Lord's wisdom and discernment. I have been truly blessed; they are already extremely successful in life. All the glory is the Lord's, who has faithfully shown me how to train up a child in the way he should go and empowered me with mercy to learn alongside of them.

One of the most powerful words of life I was given that night was my new name before the Lord, a name that identified me before the Lord. It was the greatest thing I could have ever received. I finally had an identity; I belonged to someone; I belonged to my Heavenly Father! The person I was, was no more. I was made new in every way. What was so powerful to me about all of this is that I didn't realize until later that a new name was thoroughly biblical and highly significant. God renamed many, Abram and Sarai to Abraham and Sarah,

Jacob to Israel, Simon to Peter, Saul to Paul, and now Tabetha to Mary.

The Lord called me Mary because he said I would sit at his feet and worship Him in spirit and truth, with my alabaster box. I would be one that would pour out all of my heart to Him, with my tears, at His feet. That the Lord will allow me to see His face because I genuinely love Him because He first loved me. Mary was the one that had been delivered and set free too. This is my new identity in Christ; I was called a true worshipper and a lover of His presence.

They continued to speak life and destiny over me, and they prophesied I would go home, and my husband would say, "I don't know what happened to you, but I like it!" The anger that filled my heart was transformed into the love of God in one moment in His presence; everything changed. When I walked into the house that night, I went straight home; my path had changed. I didn't need to go out with any friends; I found a true friend that would last. Jesus was all I needed. I walked into the house, and my husband took one look at me, and said, "I don't know what happened to you, but I like it." He could not quit staring into my eyes, he said, all I used to see was darkness, but now I see the light of God in your eyes. I told him all about my night. It was miraculous because it was in my eyes where I felt the demonic powers leave, and now through my eyes is where my husband can see the life of Christ.

Before I went home that night, when I arose from the place on that floor, I could barely stand because the power of God was so strong on me. I saw everything differently. I could see it clearly and accurately. I could see things that I didn't see before. I saw in the sanctuary that some had darkness over them and those that had a light. I didn't fully understand what any of it meant, but I knew I was made entirely new.

I walked over to the two witnesses who, earlier that night, had been faithful to the Lord and showed me His light. I opened my mouth, and the oracles of God flowed out. I had no clue what I was saying, but I knew God was filling my mouth with His word. I spoke that God was raising His generals for the end-time army. They both looked at me in awe and couldn't believe the power and authority I spoke in.

I had no prior knowledge of God having an end-time army or what generals of faith were. The divine knowledge came from God alone. I later realized that the army was the Lord's, and the generals were the men and women of great faith that paved the path before us. I now fully understand that the Lord was equipping me to be an overcomer and lead others into that same victory he has given me.

My life was utterly transformed; I was no longer bound to the chains of addiction, anxiety didn't have a hold on me, and depression couldn't stand anymore in the hope that I now found. When I would become afraid, I would go to the altar; when I felt lost, I would go to the altar; in everything, I learned to seek God and go to the altar. I loved to be in His presence, and every day I leaned upon His love. My feet danced with all my might; I became a vessel of freedom in the house of the Lord. I loved to worship, prophesize, and pray. I had nothing lacking in my relationship with Christ. I waited my whole life to find this firm foundation to build my life upon. My chains were gone! I had no desire for my old life because I tasted and saw the Lord was good, and that is all I ever needed.

One day in a worship service, we sang, "How great is our God," my heart was completely free, and I fully understood how great He truly is. Only God had the power to bring liberty to my life, and only God could heal the broken pieces, only God could forgive me of my sins, only God could give me a new name, only God had the love my heart so desperately needed! My whole life was changed because of Jesus's power that delivered me from a life of sin and shame.

CHAPTER 7

Restored to the Father

"I am the way and the truth and the life. No one comes to the Father except through me."

John 14:6 (NIV)

"He walks with me, and He talks with me, and He tells me I am His own, and the joy we share as we tarry there none other has ever known." The words of this song came alive in my heart; every word came true, that my savior walks with me and talks with me, and he does call me his own. That day everything had changed. The Lord had turned on the lights to my lost and hurting soul. When those lights came on, my eyes were fully opened, and I could finally see all the grace that was given to me. "Amazing grace, how sweet the sound, that saved a wretch like me, I once was lost, but now I am found, was blind, but now I see." I was no longer lost and bound; I was no longer abandoned; I could finally see the love of my Father! I was no longer striving to find acceptance in all the wrong places; I was no longer afraid; I was found and completely saved! My Father knew me because of Jesus, who made way for me! Jesus is the way, the truth, and the life, and He is the only way to the Father! Because of Jesus, I am restored to a relationship with My Heavenly Father and given true life for all eternity. *For God so loved the world that he gave His only begotten Son, that whoever believes in Him should not perish but have everlasting life,* John 3:16, NKJV. Jesus is the Father's love.

All my life, I longed to know my Father, and I remember those nights crying at my bedside, when sorrow filled my soul and my pillow filled with tears, crying out, who do I belong to? Why am I abandoned? Why does everyone that I am supposed to trust, fail to love me? Gazing at stars by night and wonder at clouds by day in hope, always wondering if Jesus was indeed there. I can now see and fully understand why the name of Jesus always made my heart leap; it was the precious Holy Spirit leading me to the only way to the Father.

As I look back on the miraculous footsteps of this journey of my life that led me to the cross of Calvary, I could see God's mighty hand upon me. My faithful Father was always with me, waiting and calling me to His arms of love and security. My heart was overwhelmed with this love and assurance, knowing that my true Father was always there. I finally realized He didn't leave me in a place of despair, He didn't abandon me, and He always provided a way to repair the broken foundations of my life.

All my life, I felt like shattered pieces, with no real sense of life or actual purpose. I wasn't strong enough to overcome the difficulties on my own or could repair what was broken. I would have never imagined that one day, I would look back and see a miraculous story, out of what I always thought of as hopeless, to be transformed into an overcoming testimony of life, and life more abundantly. Once, all I saw was broken, unmendable pieces beyond repair. I can now take a step back and see a beautiful display of all those pieces perfectly fitted in a stained-glass masterpiece that tells an incredible story that reflects a faithful Father's Love.

As a young child in church that day, when the preacher came and lifted my face and spoke that God had a plan and destiny for my life. When the song "In the Garden" etched in my heart and gave my young childlike faith hope that I could belong someday. When I look back, I can see my Father's love comforting me and calling me His own.

The day when I was on the road to rebellion, and I passed by the preacher who stood in the doors of the church on that Sunday morning and called out, *"Tabetha, are you coming in today?"* Not only was I known, but I was sought after by my Father. He never stopped calling after my prodigal heart, on the road to rebellion. His love was still pursuing me. I can now see it was my Father's love beckoning me to come into His arms that he had already provided me with a home, and all I would need was found in His arms of mercy.

The day that I stood and committed my life to a covenant of marriage before a God I hadn't truly known but knew me. Who blessed me with the greatest blessing of my life, a husband that would lead my heart to Calvary? A loving, devoted, and patient husband who would become my greatest companion. Although I had dropped the ring, and I was afraid, my Father spoke life over me and said, "She will drop this, but just like in life, she will pick it back up." My Father knew every wrong that I would ever make, yet he still knew I would find my way to His grace to empower me to overcome every difficult place. My Father's love had an amazing plan to bring true redemption to my life. He provided a way for me to be made whole. He saw me as complete, even when I was still broken, lost, afraid, and ashamed. I pray that you will know this love of the Father, that even in our weaknesses, He still sees His Son's sacrifice of love, and He calls us his very own.

At David's grandmother's bedside, He gently encouraged me to tell the truth and reminded me of the letter. The letter was God's word that He wrote for all of us, revealing the truth of who He is and how He loves us and has a plan and purpose for everyone. His word is life and shows us what path is right. His word is the truth, and the truth that sets us free.

In the word of God, when Jesus was on the cross of Calvary, the thief next to him asked the Lord to remember Him when he came into his Kingdom. Jesus said, "Even this day, you will be with me in paradise." When the Lord spoke to me in that room with grandma, He said, "I will remember you." The miracle is that the Lord declared that my name will be written in my lamb's book of life forever. I will not forget you. I will not leave you as an orphan; I will not forsake you; I will remember you.

After I finally came to the place of Calvary, and I understood it is the place of surrendering everything I am to God's only begotten Son, so that I could become everything I was created to be. A place of great faith and true love, to receive a grace that I so desperately need. A place of complete forgiveness, and with a priceless exchange, His life for mine to be set free. My Father paid my debt with His only Son to be renamed and called His very own. It wasn't the Father's fault man had chosen another way and fallen into a life of sin. But He is faithful to provide us with a way of redemption, and the price was His very own Son. God's love gave us the ultimate sacrifice. It was the highest price to pay. God has always given us a choice. He never forces us to choose His will or way because He is good. However, He is faithful to provide us with all we need to be reconciled to Him. Oh, how He longs for us to choose life. He patiently waits and beckons us to come to life. He watches down our prodigal roads, longing for us to come into His truth and return home.

How could it be that Jesus paid it all for me so that I would be redeemed, oh my heart, burns this powerful love within me? Every step of the way, my Father has provided for me. He knows my name! I am alive in Him! The peace that washes over my soul, knowing my Father loves me, no other joy I will ever know! I have a Father that I can run to in every heartache, and He reminds me that I am his and never to be afraid. I have a Father that loves me. In His arms, I am safe, secured, and made completely whole. He guides me, and He provides for me; He leads me alongside His still waters and restores my soul. My Father is Jesus's Father and is the Father of us all, the creator of life, the one true living God forever.

IDENTITY

My identity has been restored. I am no longer an orphan with no name, with a missing father. Or a product of the hands of abuse. I am no longer bound by addiction. I am no longer searching for love in all the wrong places. My name has been changed, and I am adopted, I am found, I am His. I have a new life, a Father who has provided all that I will ever need through the love and sacrifice of His Son. Growing in the understanding that God will never leave me nor forsake me was the most significant revelation to who my Father is. My Father's love doesn't reject me, hurt me, or condemn me. His love has given me the acceptance that I always longed for. I now know who I am. I am His daughter, and I carry after His image. He has made all things new in me. The word tells us to behold old things have passed away, and He makes all things new. He is a father to the fatherless; He has made us His people and has chosen us and created us after His very own likeness after His Son. He said that we were predestined to be conformed to the image of Christ. He put a new spirit within us, His spirit. His life, My Father's life, is living inside me. We are sealed and marked as His until the day of redemption.

Identity is a beautiful thing; it is what marks you, what characteristics make you, you. The Father took everything that identified me as what I was, lost, broken, and full of sin, and replaced it with everything He is, by the power of the blood of Jesus that has completely redeemed me. I now have the fruit of His life and likeness that identifies me as His. How beautiful, all just because I came to a place of true surrender, received this life that was given to me, by grace and through faith, I am His. I believed and received, and now I am living a new life, with a new birth certificate that has been forever documented in the lamb's book of life, my name is written.

My new identity as a redeemed child of God has given me powerful access to the provisions of my Father. Remember, in the beginning, I spoke about how your identity gives you access to the necessities of life? A Father's love provides for his children. One significant provision I have is to know my Father's love and comfort. Everything I need is found in His arms of love. I know I am safe; I know I am provided for. His provision of love covers everything. Where I used to live in constant lack, I now have an abundance of overflow. When I need anything, I run to my Father. He doesn't deny me; He provides for me. When I need grace, I can come to Him and receive mercy in my need. When I need forgiveness, He is faithful to forgive and cleanse me of all unrighteousness. When I need shelter from harm, He covers me with His wings of protection. When I need strength, He empowers me in my weakness. When I need wisdom and direction, He gives it to me liberally and guides me every step of the way. When I need healing for my body, by His stripes, I am already healed. He has given me all that I will ever need. When I need understanding, He gives it to me. He never condemns me or refuses to listen; He is always there. A faithful Father indeed.

PROVISION & PROTECTION

His provision provides the protection I need from all my enemies. He anoints my head with oil in the presence of my enemies. Before I knew Calvary, my enemy had tormented, abused, taken advantage of me, and overcame me. I was powerless. I had to fight with my strength, my understanding, in my ability. My enemies were too strong for me. I had lost many battles. My Father's love has provided victory after victory over every enemy. He has caused me to become an overcomer! I am no longer fighting from a place of survival but seated in a position of overcoming victory. Because "It is finished."

Yes, there are still battles I face, but my Father has the victory. He gives me His strength and His weapons that are mighty to pull down the strongholds. I no longer have to fight the way I used to. There are some days that I forget, and I attempt to fight in my ability and strength, leaning on my understanding, and when I am wounded and weary, I run to my Father's arms, and He reminds me, "It is finished." He counsels me and faithfully reminds me that I am not fighting alone or from a place for victory, but a place of victory. Hallelujah! He is my victory! Glory! The rest of our souls when we rest fully in Christ's provision and protection alone.

DIRECTION & CORRECTION

My Father's love always guides me. He always shows me the path that is right for me. He never leaves me wondering or confused about the direction to go. His word is a light to my feet; it directs every choice I need to make. I have learned many times I am waiting for direction, but He never leaves me in a state of wondering for direction. He gives me a choice and helps me along the way. Sometimes I miss it; I didn't realize that I made a wrong turn. But I quickly run back to the arms of my Father, and He shows me the right path.

Life is a journey full of places to go and decisions to make, and sometimes we can get lost along that way. Go off on our own, not realizing we have wandered away. Sometimes we lean on our understanding, and that can get us in a ruff place. His faithful word tells us not to rely on our knowledge, but in all ways acknowledge Him, and He will direct our path. When we find ourselves searching for the right way to go and lean on our Father's love, He will never fail to point us in the right direction and lead us through every season to a place of His perfect destiny.

My favorite about my Father's love is His loving correction. I don't know where I would be, had it not been for His great love that corrects me. I love that my Father doesn't ever let me ever get too far away from His purpose and path. There have been many times that I have missed it, and I have failed. I have become undone even after coming into this new life; it is still a journey. I have found great comfort in My Father's correction. He loves me enough to correct me and guide me into the path of life. He has shown me many things through the years, how to handle life's stresses, complicated situations, how to steer clear from the traps of the enemy, how to guard my heart, how to overcome every season in His love. How to remain in Him, and commit to your word, like He does His. He has shown me how to abide in His love and the power of prayer and humility. He shows me the importance of integrity in everything we do. He keeps my heart from selfish pride. He corrects me to create in me his character and nature that will stand the test of time. When I mess up and fall, His grace empowers me to overcome. I found that sitting at His feet is a place of constant dependency, and that is where I will be all of the days of my life.

I love my Father's correction because it never rejects me, condemns me, accuses me, blames me, or attacks me. He just lovingly corrects me, and once I learn and repent, I overcome. His correction empowers me to live righteously. Sometimes I have had to learn a few lessons a time or two because I am still me, and there are weaknesses in my humanity, but through the trials and, yes, the sufferings, He is establishing me and is making me perfect by His love.

Correction doesn't always feel good, but I am assured it is working out for my good in my Father's love. That is why I love it, receive it, and cling to it. My everyday prayer is, Father create a clean heart in me and continually renew the right spirit within me. A life of humility and repentance that can admit its needs and wrongs is a life that is dependent on Him entirely; it keeps us from a life of pride and reaches towards the mark of Christ, hungering and thirsting for what is right.

PURPOSE

My Father's love fills my life with all my needs. It makes me entirely complete, nothing missing, and nothing broken. He has healed every broken piece and will continue to restore my life until the day I am with Him face to face. Jesus said, "You should rejoice for me because I am going to be with my Father." When He ascended into heaven, He was going to a much greater place, a place of fullness of love and power to sit at the right hand of the Father and make perfect intercession for us. I understand with my whole heart, Jesus's longing to be with the Father. He said greater things would you do, know that I go, it is better that I go because I will pray to the Father that will send you another comforter, that will empower you to fulfill God's will and purpose in life.

We each have a unique purpose that we were created for, and the Father knows exactly what each one of us is destined to do. He knows why he made us and the plans and the purpose he has for us. Remember, when someone truly knows their true identity in the Father's love, they will fully know their purpose. That is because when we know who our Father truly is and who we belong to, we will know what we were created for. Jesus finished his path of purpose. He was always connected in the perfect relationship with the Father. Jesus's focus was to fulfill the will of the Father. Jesus said I don't do or say anything unless I hear or see my Father do or say it. He said if you have seen me, you have seen the Father. Jesus revealed who the Father truly is to us, remember he told us have I been with you so long that you don't see the Father? The Father is in me, and I in the Father. At the garden of Gethsemane, Jesus prayed, "Father, not my will but yours be done." Jesus's life was to fulfill the Father's purpose, and you see the fruit of his surrendered life to the Father. Jesus loved the Father. He lived for the Father; in everything He did, He did it for the Father.

Jesus said the same way the Father has sent me, now I send you. Jesus fulfilling his purpose in the Father empowers us to run our race and continue the purpose of the Father's love in the world. We have been reconciled and are the children of God, representing our Heavenly Father, and each of us has a unique divine purpose to fulfill in the Father's love. Just as Jesus is in this world, so are we. Before Jesus ascended to the Father, He told Mary in John 20:17, "Go to my brothers and tell them I am ascending to My Father and Your father and to My God and your God." The powerful truth in the words of Jesus was the relationship He had with God as Father is made available through Him so that we all could all be reconciled to a relationship with the Father. Jesus called us brothers! That means we are in a new family; the powerful exchange of sin has changed our identity and nature for righteousness on the cross of Calvary. Jesus revealed the Father's love to us, made it available, finished his course, and opened the gates of heaven to restore us. He restored us to a relationship with Our Heavenly Father.

"But as many as received Him, to them He gave the right to become children of God, to those who believe in His name. Who were born, not of blood, nor of the will of the flesh, nor of the will of man, but of God."

John 1:12-13 (NKJV)

CHAPTER 8

Growing in Relationship

It has been an incredible journey. I pray that as I share my story with you, you can not only see the mighty, loving hand of God in my life but with you as well! He is a faithful Father to us all, and I know at times in life, it can seem like you are without comfort, without love, or the assurance of God's steadfast devotion for you. But I am here to testify that you can count on Him! He is for you, not against you, and His love is real. Just the same way God made a miraculous way for me, He has made way for you. My story is unique to my life, but your story is special to yours. We all have a unique purpose, and we are all created to know the Love of the Father, in Christ Jesus. I want to encourage you that you are special, you are loved, and you are highly valuable. It doesn't matter what sin has done; God's love and power are faithful to cleanse you and restore you completely! I promise you the same transformative power that God delivered me with; He has given us all. It is found at the cross of Calvary. Keep seeking the truth, and you will find the truth, and the truth will set you free!

I wanted to share some keys that I have learned over the years walking with God as my Father. Some of the lessons I have learned come through long hard seasons of discovering my new life in Christ. I had to endure a lot, learn a lot, and still do. But I would love to share with you the truths of walking with God in a relationship that has helped me see my Father's love in my everyday life.

LOVE

When you think of a relationship, what is the key component of any relationship? It is love! You cannot have a real relationship without love; it is impossible. Love is the foundation of a relationship; without it, there would be no genuine devotion. After coming into my new life in Christ, the first thing that happened was the love of God filled my heart, and it replaced all the fear and anger; it healed the pain of trauma, it secured me in everlasting hope. This love was so powerful that it caused me to love even my enemies! It was impossible to hate; His love is so powerful it healed my heart and caused all my enemies of addiction and affliction to flee. I want to reflect on the scripture of John 3:16 NKJV, most people have heard and know this scripture, and most Christians reflect on it, but I want to understand that this scripture is much more than a reciting verse is the foundation to everything that God is.

"For God so *loved* the world.... that He gave.....His only begotten Son...that whoever believes in Him..... should not perish....but... have everlasting life..." John 3:16 (NKJV)

Allow that truth to rest in your heart. Before I knew God, I had always wondered what He was like. I always longed to know. Some people see Him as a hard rule bearing, high standard, judging God. We all have heard it before, some people say, if I ever go to church, the roof will cave in because of all the wrong I have done. They instantly see their inability to be perfect, their sin, and conclude that God would reject them. Once I had someone tell me that I would go to hell for my lifestyle. I remember hearing those words over the phone and thought, well, I don't know how to be any other way, this is all I know, and I guess I have no hope. I felt the fear of rejection and knew that I wasn't good enough. The truth is we all fall short of the glory of God.

We need to re-read that scripture again.

"For God so *loved* the world that He *gave* His only begotten Son that *whoever* believes in Him should not perish but have everlasting life" John 3:16 (NKJV).

One of the greatest mistakes people make is they don't see God for who He truly is. In 1 John 4:8, the scripture says God is love! God is love! That is His nature; He is perfect love! The perfect love that knows your sin and provides a way of redemption by simply believing and receiving that through Jesus, your sins that you fear will cause the roof to cave in, are forgiven if you put your heart to believe for God so loved the world. Trust that the life of sin you are stuck in, God will empower you to overcome by believing and receiving it is finished at the cross of Calvary, and the resurrection to new life.

God is a relational God. He longs to be reconciled to you; that is why Jesus has paid the price for our sin and is the road to redemption to new life. We are created for a relationship with God; apart from God, we are lost, broken, and left with a great void in our lives. Remember, the Father's love is the foundation for all of us. It establishes so much security in our lives because it is how we are truly designed to live, a life connected to the creator of life, our Heavenly Father. There is no real peace apart from being reconciled to the Father. It is impossible to have peace without reconciliation to a relationship with Jesus, the prince of peace himself. Jesus is the only way to the Father.

GROWING IN LOVE

In my walk with God, learning about His love didn't happen overnight. Yes, I had an amazing life-giving encounter with God that changed me forever. But learning about His love is still a growing process. In life, I was let down so much that I had a lot of insecurities in my soul that would always tend to rise in my heart in moments of adversity, challenge, or uncertainty. I would find myself in cycles of what if? What if I fall short? Will He still love me? What if I miss it? Will He always carry me? What if my inability to be entirely perfect and mature in all my ways causes me to fail in this new life I was given? What if I don't make it? What if? I am completely transparent with you; these feelings and thoughts are things that try to take root to keep you in a state of fear. The truth is perfect love casts out all fear! The same way God loved me yesterday is the same way He will continue to love me today and forever. God's love is patient; it is kind. He is rich in mercy; He is long in suffering. God's love is enduring. His love never fails; it never ends! He will continue to love us despite all of our weaknesses, failures, fears.

I am not saying, do whatever you want because God's love will never change so that you can live however you feel and take for granted God's precious grace that was paid for us at the ultimate high cost. What I am saying is in those moments when you feel you missed it so bad that God couldn't forgive you because the guilt and condemnation are so heavy on your soul, trust in His love for you. God's love will always forgive you; He didn't send his Son to condemn you but to bring you true liberty in His love.

GUILT & CONDEMNATION

I will share a story with you that will reveal how the enemy of your soul will use guilt and condemnation to cloud your understanding of God's love for you. Several years after my salvation, I fell into a hard time. I experienced some tough hurtful situations in the church that led me to *feel* alone, depressed, and separated from God's love. I had experienced the hardship of church hurt, and it devastated me as a new Christian. The church was my home and everything I longed for my whole life, and that disappointment of hurt was enough to cloud my perception, cause me to distrust, and hinder my understanding of God's love. To me, the church was an extension of the Father's love in the Earth, and that it is! But the church is also a work in progress, a place that the enemy is continually warring against and trying to operate through to corrupt and discredit God's people's credibility to keep us from coming to the saving knowledge of Christ. In my early years of walking with God, I did not fully realize this. So, the enemy took advantage of my lack of knowledge and tried to utilize people's imperfections to cloud my perception of a perfect loving Father.

Back to the story, after I had experienced this devastation in my life, I made some awful decisions. I went back to the ways of my past for a brief moment. The enemy came back and knocked at the door with his false comfort and deception. I was ignorant enough to fall into his trap. After he successfully distorted my vision of the church, through hurt, he came as a false comfort in what used to bring me relief. It was the most devastating time in my life. For several weeks, I walked a path that I was once delivered from. I returned to the place of my sin. It only lasted briefly, before I came to my senses and repentance. But it happened; the conflict that continued was great. The wage of my sin caused me three in half years of deep depression. Why? Was God punishing me for my sin? No! But that is what I thought. You see, I was now under a cloud of guilt and condemnation. I couldn't forgive myself for falling into the temptations of sin after being born again. It devastated me. Because all I ever wanted was my Father, and knowing that I knew Him, I fell away from Him, and in that, I couldn't bring myself to forgive myself.

The issue was, I didn't have the full knowledge of God's love for me. I believed the lie that I would never get back to the life-giving relationship I had because I was deceived enough to fall into sin. The root of the issue was I was struggling in my soul with the fear of abandonment and rejection. My spirit was born again, but my mind still needed to be renewed to the truth! The truth that God said, He will never leave me nor forsake me! For three in half years, I struggled. I was at war with myself and the enemy of my soul. I thought, after everything God did for me, this is how I act? I should have known better. I should have made better decisions. What kind of testimony is this? You got all your prayers answered, and then you fell away out of disappointment and pain? God can never restore to you what you had because you left it. That was the lie that filled my thoughts for years. I became afraid to go to church. Not because I was fearful of God, I loved God with all my heart! The feeling of disappointing the one I loved the most caused me great feelings of despair. I was afraid to go to church because of what I faced in that hurt, betrayal, mistrust, and the abuse that took place. Was it a safe place? I was afraid to let my walls down again. I was afraid to trust again.

I have shared this because I want to expose the lies that once trapped me for years! The truth is, I was forgiven! God's word says He is faithful and just to forgive us and cleanse us from all unrighteousness. I asked for forgiveness. I didn't continue in the sin; I repented; I was genuinely sorry for it. That was the truth I needed to know that set me free from the fear of unforgiveness. God's love for me was more powerful than the enemy's plan to take me out by sin and by the guilt of the sin. I could be restored! After several years, I finally understood the lies I was believing and began to see the truth of God's love for me. I recognized the enemy's devices, and I learned to discern the voice of truth through the renewing of my mind. I realized the awestruck truth; nothing can separate me from the love of God that is in Christ Jesus. Nothing. I still had a Heavenly Father who loved me and who had forgiven me. He did not abandon me in my weakest moment of sin; He was still covering me and calling me His! The moment that I said I was sorry was the moment I was forgiven. I didn't have to live in guilt for all those years. All I needed to do is shake it off, get back in the race, and fight the good fight of faith!

Think about it, if you are learning to ride a bike, and you are trying your best, and fall, not intending to fall, but you do. Does your Father who is holding you up and instructing you condemn, yell at you, and disown you? No! He comes running after you! He picks you up! He puts you back on the bike and says, do it again! Do it again! Do it again! Keep pedaling! Don't stop! Don't look back! Keep your eyes fixed straight ahead! He bandages up your wounds, instructs you, and keeps you pushing to overcome! That is the love of a Father! I had to learn that was the truth! Once I realized, I overcame the weight of guilt and condemnation!

Just like the prodigal son, the prodigal son left the Father's house, spent his inheritance on wild living and partying. He went down the wrong road and made some bad choices. However, the Father's love was always longing for His son to return. He watched down His prodigal road, waiting for His son's return. He was not looking to condemn His son but restore His son. When the son finally came to his end, he knew that even his Father's servants were treated better than the life of pig's food, he returned home. He did not return with pride in his heart but returned in true humility and repentance. He was more than content with being a servant, but the Father restored him as his rightful son. He placed the ring on his finger and rob on his shoulders. He clothed him, rejoiced over him, and restored him in the Father's love.

Romans 8:1, NKJV, *There is therefore now no condemnation to those who are in Christ Jesus, who do not walk according to the flesh, but according to the Spirit.* I was forgiven, yesterday, tomorrow, and forever! The scripture says in 1 John 4:19, KJV, We love Him because He first loved us. This love is so powerful. We have to spend our lives living out this truth, for God so loved the world He gave His only begotten Son that whosoever believes in him will not perish but have everlasting life! God's love empowers us to live righteously, wholly, completely before Him. I said love is the foundation of every relationship, and I had to realize the depths of the love of God. The same forgiveness that ransomed me was the same forgiveness that would follow me all of the days of my life. His love didn't change; it remained the same.

Growing in the truth of the love of God is a lifelong journey. It will continue until the day I see Him face to face. Jesus said in Matthew 22:37-39, NLT, *You must love the Lord your God with all your heart, all your soul, and all your mind. This is the first and greatest commandment. A second is equally important: love your neighbor as yourself.* I have found that growing in your understanding of God's love is the foundational truth to your relationship with Him, and once you realize how true His love is, you will walk in complete confidence in Him and who you are as His child. You won't fall into temptations as easily when you realize the truth. You walk in godly confidence that Christ finished Calvary's work and is all you need to set your eyes upon.

Once you know His love for you personally and intimately, you will love others the same way He has loved you. Jesus said in John 13:35, NLT, *Your love for one another will prove to the world that you are my disciples.* It is the goodness of God that leads men to repentance! Knowing His love and goodness is what sets us free from the temptations of sin and the heavy burdens of guilt! Knowing our identity, purpose, and God's faithfulness is the key to walking in lasting victory over sin!

LEARNING TO TRUST

Just like love is a foundation for any relationship, so is trust. Trust is essential for a healthy functioning relationship. Remember, a relationship is between two people. One cannot have a relationship with oneself; it is a union, a togetherness. Picture a three-legged race; you have two separate people whose right and left legs are joined as one. Each person has to do their part to move forward as one step together. That is how I see a relationship; it is joined, together, mended. A healthy relationship is founded in love, and trust propels a productive relationship.

Love ties you together, but trust is what moves you forward. If you don't trust the one you are in relation with, you won't be willing to submit to one another, you won't allow yourself to be vulnerable, and you will refuse to be honest and transparent. Think about it, you can't walk unless you trust the other one is entirely for you, and you can genuinely rely on them to do their part. A relationship is a function; it is a powerful movement. It is why relationships are to be chosen wisely;

you don't want to get joined to the wrong one. But that is for another lesson.

Today let's focus on the trust it takes to have a healthy relationship with our Heavenly Father.

PETER, DO YOU TRUST ME?

My heart is reminded of Peter, who, after Jesus was arrested, denied ever knowing Jesus three times. What could have been going on in Peter's heart that day? Peter loved the Lord. Peter was the only one that stepped out of the boat and walked on water with Jesus! But Peter also started to sink when he focused on the waves. When Peter called out to the Lord, Jesus reached down and saved him, and said, "You of little faith, why did you doubt?" (Matthew 14:31) You see, I think Jesus was speaking to a bigger issue on the inside of Peter. Why did you doubt? Doubt is the opposite of trust. Faith works by love, and love is faithful. Love is true. You can trust the love of God.

When Jesus was having his last supper with Peter, He once again spoke to the root in Peter of doubt. He told Peter, you will deny me three times, on this very night. Peter, full of zeal, full of desire, full of passion, had a root that needed healing. I love that the Lord never disqualified Peter for his weakness; He just revealed it and then ultimately healed it. It was through the testing and trial that Peter had learned the shortcomings of his zealous faith even when he cut the ear of the soldier off to defend the Lord; it could not measure up to the simplicity of an unwavering trust in his relationship with the Lord. When he realized he had denied the Lord three times that night, his heart was sorrowful.

Jesus, after the resurrection, came to Peter and broke bread with Him. He said three times; Peter, do you love me? Peter, do you love me? Peter, do you love me? Peter, yes, Lord, I love you. Let's replace the word love with trust. Love and trust are so closely related. Peter, do you trust me? Peter, do you trust me? Peter, do you trust me? You see, love must operate in trust. Jesus told the disciples all that would take place before it did. But did the disciples trust that he would rise again? Did Peter trust that he would not sink? Did he trust the Lord with all his heart?

Proverbs 3:5, NLT, says, *Trust in the Lord with all your heart, do not depend on your own understanding.* Peter was faced with a great question; do you love me? Do you trust me? Peter's zeal brought him out unto those waters when his eyes were fixed on Jesus, he walked! Jesus was displaying and building a record with Peter, showing Peter, Peter, you can trust me! Remember the waters? Remember when I told you, you would deny me? Remember when I told you I would rise? Remember my faithfulness! Remember, the words I have spoken to you are true, and you can trust me!

Yet it is still ultimately Peter's choice to trust Jesus; it is his choice to walk in the union of the relationship of trust. Peter's part is to trust Jesus wholeheartedly in his relationship with the Lord. A lot like Peter, we all have those moments and places in us that the Lord will reveal His faithfulness, even when we are ye of little faith. The faithfulness of God is trustworthy! He is the truth itself! I am the way the truth and the life! We can trust him!

It takes time to develop this trust in a relationship. Once you establish a track record of experiences that you can look back on, you will grow stronger and stronger in trusting the Lord. The Lord does not need to earn our trust because He alone is true! But His love is so tender that He walks with us as we develop genuine lasting confidence with Him. Can you trust Him with your disappointments? Can you trust Him with your failings? Can you trust Him with all your heart, not leaning on your own understanding? That is the heart the Lord wants from us; He wants us to believe and trust in Him. Did it make any sense in our human thinking to walk on water? No, it doesn't. But in Jesus, it makes perfect sense! That is the kind of trust we need to walk in. When the Lord tells you to do something, trust that His word is true!

I struggled for several years with trust. Remember, I came from a place that every father figure abandoned or abused me. Then I was healed from that place and put into another season of hurt and abuse in a church family. Dealing with the church hurt and disappointments, I thought can I trust this? I still was faced with great adversity in my faith, and I had to choose what I would trust? The truth was I did love the Lord like Peter; I walked on water, I stood up for Him in zealous acts, but when that moment came, I sank because I took my eyes off of trusting the Lord even in the challenge. But God was always faithful. At every step of the way, no matter the situation, He proved to me, that yes daughter, you can trust me!

TRUSTING THE FATHER WITH MY SON

I will tell you a story that took great courage and trust. It was one of the most challenging times of my life. I had learned God's faithfulness through the difficult times, and I will display that to you. Several years ago, my middle son had an operation. He had his tonsils removed. It was supposed to be a simple procedure, and it was. We brought him home the same day. For several days, we cared for him and nursed him back to health. After ten days, the doctors said Joshua could return to school. It was that day, and I had a feeling in my stomach he wasn't ready to go, but I went ahead with the doctor's orders to send him.

Joshua returned to school, and I was resting on the couch. I worked two part-time jobs to help pay for the children's Christian education, and I was exhausted after caring for Joshua and all I had to do. Since the surgery, Josh was at school for the first time, and I had a minute to myself. Laying on the couch, trying to rest, and resist the urges of fear of Joshua returning to school too soon, my phone rang. "Mrs. Henderson, you need to come here; Joshua is bleeding, we are not sure what to do, he went to the water fountain, and a significant amount of blood filled the fountain, he is pale, we gave him an ice pack for his neck." My heart sank like Peter in the water. I jumped up and said, "I am on my way immediately!"

I was so afraid! I was shaken! I knew it was serious. I called the doctor on my way to pick Joshua up, and they said to get him to the emergency room. I drove faster than an ambulance, I am telling you, I could not get there fast enough. When I got to the school, I ran up the stairs into the office, and saw my son, paler than I had ever seen him before, he was extremely out of it, no energy at all, it seemed like he was in and out. The office personnel looked at me with great concern. I said he doesn't look good at all, they agreed. I honestly can't remember how I got him in the car, but I did. And I drove faster than before. My son felt lifeless; he was drifting off in the passenger side seat. I kept shouting, "Joshua!

Joshua! You stay with me; you stay with me!" Because he was passing out.

I got him to the hospital, and this began a seven-day journey of great trials. His blood pressure was low, and the doctors confirmed he had a bleed. They could not determine how much blood he lost because it was well in the water fountain, and the spot that was bleeding had stopped, for now. They advised us to continue soft foods, keep a watch for it, and say ice would restrict bleeding. So, the ice pack was a brilliant move at the school. With nothing much to do, they sent us home, hoping Joshua's body would heal on its own. Going back in and cauterizing the bleed could cause a more significant bleeding problem and risk for infection, so it was much safer to do it this way.

We returned home, and within the same night, Joshua bled again. Back to the hospital, we went, and back home, we were sent. For the entire week, this is what continues to happen. He would bleed, it would stop, we would get released. It was terrible. There was nothing we could do but trust that he would be okay. Every time we went to the doctors, they sent us home. All the while, I knew he wasn't improving; he was getting worse. It was visible. I was doing all I knew how to do, and still, it wasn't enough. I was praying all the prayers I could pray, and yet, I couldn't find the comfort of faith and love. I was afraid I was losing my son. I could see he wasn't healing correctly. Each day he would get weaker and was still on a restricted diet, so the blood and nutrients he lost were tough to replace. When I was bathing him, he was thanking me and told me how nice it felt just to get cleaned up after running back and forth to the hospital. Suddenly, he became very slack and began to pass out right in my arms. I scooped him up and ran down the stairs and called for my husband. I lifted Joshua's feet in the air and took his blood pressure as I kept urgently calling for him to keep his eyes open. His blood pressure was dangerously low, so back to the hospital we went. They admitted Joshua, and I was relieved!

I thought maybe this time, they would figure it out, and he would mend! I had my husband spend the night with him, so I can go home and get on my knees and cry out to God. I cried out in anguish, God, please, please heal my son! Please, Lord, show me what to do! Tell me it is going to be okay! The whole night I cried in prayer, hoping to feel the relief of God's presence bring peace to this stormy sea, as I felt like I was watching my son's life slip away! He was bleeding slowly, and no one could stop it but God.

While at the hospital, Joshua almost passed out again in the bathroom. His body was weak, and his blood pressure was low. They continued to treat him with IV fluids, and the doctor advised us again that she could not perform surgery; it would be too risky. She assured us that he would pull through, that it was rare this was happening and asked if he had any bleeding disorders, to which he did not. Once again, the doctor said time would heal. We got sent home.

That night Joshua was home. He no longer looked pale but green; his skin had a terrible tint to it. I was sick over this. I was afraid, and I kept trying my best to help him get back to health. Joshua was worried. Every time he closed his eyes, he would panic and think he was bleeding. That night I had Joshua sleep on the couch, and I laid on the floor, on a mattress in the living room. It was too much to keep going up the steps with a sick child. So, I thought we had better stay on the first floor.

I woke up sometime after midnight; I couldn't sleep. My mind was alert and watching over my son. I heard Joshua groaning in some discomfort. He cried out, my belly, my belly hurts! I went to comfort him and told him it was okay. He said, "I think I am bleeding." I checked and saw a few trickles. I did what the doctors instructed me to do; I had him suck on ice to constrict the blood vessels. They told us all week if it is a trickle, you are fine. If he is vomiting up piles of blood, get him back here immediately.

I ensured Joshua he would be okay and tried my best to get him to rest. The next thing I know, he yelled out a great cry of distress and vomited piles of blood all over the living room! I scooped him up and cried out to my husband to call 911! Call 911! Joshua was passing out in my arms for the third time this week; this time, I knew his little body had enough! He was struggling to hang on, he was afraid, he was lifeless, his body had been through an ongoing traumatic trauma for several weeks, and it would not stop! The ambulance came; I was able to keep Joshua awake. His blood pressure was 80/30, he was green, he was weak, and he was stricken with a great affliction. They took him to the hospital by ambulance, and my husband went with him.

All week long, I was on edge, driving as fast as I could, alert, in emergency mode, I was in fight mode. Fighting for my son's life, doing all I could do to keep him alive. At this moment, I am not sure if it was shock or what, but I couldn't move fast at all. I had to clean up my son's blood, get the other kids up for school, and make my way to the hospital. Maybe I was in shock because I didn't know what would happen. Perhaps I was just stricken with fear. It was the absolute worst feeling in the world, knowing that I could lose my precious son.

I walked to the car, got the kids all packed up. Felt like a slow-motion picture. I was frozen in time. I put my keys in the ignition and lifted my last prayer; I was done fighting; I did not know what to do. I felt helpless. I had to surrender this to the Father. I prayed, "God, whether Joshua is with you or with me, we have the victory. I love my son, and I don't want to lose him. It would be terrible grief that I am not sure how I would bear. But I know that if he is with you in heaven, he would be a lot happier with you. It's perfect with you; he wouldn't be in pain. He would be forever free. I would love for you to allow him to be with me, but I will trust you no matter if he is with you or me, I will trust you. We have the victory. I surrender Joshua to you, Lord. I trust you." At that very moment, I finally felt the comfort of the Lord, not that He wasn't faithful to comfort me all week. It was just in that moment I finally quit fighting in my strength and surrendered my will, my son, my understanding, and my trust in the Father. I released it. I released my son to the will of God. No matter the outcome, I was determined I would trust the Lord with the result.

Supernatural peace washed over me. I felt the love of the Father fill my heart with peace that Joshua would be okay. I knew it! I called my husband, and I told him I have this incredible peace that everything will turn around. My husband said while he was in the ambulance, he had a supernatural peace come over him, and he knew the Lord was assuring him, it would be okay. Joshua's blood levels were so low at the hospital that they couldn't get an IV in, and they couldn't draw any blood out. They eventually did, discovered he had lost half of his body's blood volume, and sent him life transport to a better hospital that could better handle his care. They advised us that if Joshua bled one more time at the new hospital, his heart and lungs wouldn't be able to take that kind of strain. It was a life-threatening situation. He needed a blood transfusion; we agreed and permitted the procedure. However, Joshua reacted to the transfusion, and they had to stop it abruptly. He didn't get much blood. That night, we had to pray the bleeding would stop, and Joshua would not have a severe reaction to the transfusion. We all waited.

It was the first night Joshua had not bled! We got through the first night! It was the first breakthrough all week! The second night, no bleeding! The third night no bleeding! Joshua's bleeding miraculously stopped! He was finally healing! The relief and thanksgiving in our hearts was overwhelming. We knew the hand of God saved our son that year. We finally got discharged and were sent home a day before Christmas eve!

I learned a great truth in my life that God is truly one you can trust! There isn't any other person or thing in this world that deserves the trust that belongs to the true one. God is faithful, He is true, and you can trust Him in every situation no matter the result. If bad things happen, He will turn it around for good. He works all things together for good to those that love Him and are called according to His purpose. Whether we see how God will turn it around and use it doesn't matter, we have to trust that He is good and faithful and will do all He said He would!

After that, I was able to look back and see all the places God has been faithful to me. Every difficulty He turned around. Every trail He saw me through. He has never left me and nor forsaken me. I started to realize God wants my trust, He longs for me to know He is for me, not against me, and He is committed to me. I can call upon His name, and He will deliver me from destruction. He is my help in time of need. He is my direction in the valley. He is my faithful Father, who is devoted to me. I felt like Abraham with Isaac, who had to trust God for the sacrifice.

I felt a glimpse of what it was to watch the priceless exchange of your son's blood for the sins of the world. Watching my son bleed, suffer, in pain with his life slowly leaving his body. It helped me see even more the price of Calvary. God gave us His Son and had to watch as He suffered for the sins of the word so we could be free. I am not saying that I know exactly how God felt to surrender His Son for us. But I do have a better understanding of the price, the cost, and the love it took. The Father gave me the greatest gift that Christmas Eve; He gave me my son, because He had already provided His so that we would all live.

KEYS TO RELATIONSHIP

Walking in a relationship takes love, trust, devotion, and time. I have had many seasons and valleys to walk through, and every time I can tell you God is faithful and true. I learned that if I focused on the true nature of God, I would never doubt His love for me. I would always know His goodness. Scripture says goodness and mercy will follow me all the days of my life. It has taken many, many years to build my heart with the understanding of the truth.

Once, the Lord spoke to me and said, you need to know that I am good. You keep doubting my goodness. You are wavering in fear and uncertainty. You have to learn to trust my goodness. The Lord was right. Whenever a challenging situation happened, and I got another outcome that I didn't expect, I somehow shrunk back in uncertainty. When I started to stand on His love, goodness, and faithfulness, I quit shrinking back and began to rise in confidence.

In understanding the love of God, we cannot solely see grace and not rightfully divide that He is holy and just. I never failed or sinned, knowing I could just be forgiven; that would be taking advantage of God's love and grace. God's love empowers us to love Him with wholehearted devotion. I don't pray because I have to. I pray because I want to spend time with my loving Father. I don't restrain from unrighteousness living because I have to; I do it because I love my Father more than anything else. When you wholeheartedly devote yourself to love God, you will find your heart already doing what is right because it flows from a heart that's hungering and thirsting for righteousness. In today's Christianity, there is a misconception that it is "religious" to stay free from the world's desires and be devoted to a life of prayer and steadfast commitment to living righteously. I have to say it is not "religious" it is love and wholehearted devotion. When you truly walk in the love of God, you walk in obedience to God. Jesus said, if you love me, obey me. Peter, do you trust me? Then feed my sheep. Jesus called for Peter's obedience after he confirmed his love for Jesus. Love always takes action.

CHAPTER 9

Guarding Your Heart

*The thief does not come except to steal, and to kill,
and to destroy. I have come that they may have life,
and that they may have it more abundantly.*

John 10:10 (NKJV)

THE SEED OF THE WORD OF GOD

Jesus told us a parable about the seed of the Word of God. He taught us what happens to the seed after it's planted in our hearts and warned us of the things to guard our hearts against. Walking in my new life in Christ, I have learned the truths of God's Word and learned that protecting your heart is essential to keeping the Word of God producing life and life more abundantly in your life.

Jesus spoke in John 8:5-8 NKJV,

A sower went out to sow his seed. And as he sowed, some fell by the wayside; and it was trampled down, and the birds of the air devoured it. Some fell on rock; and as soon as it sprang up, it withered away because it lacked moisture. And some fell among thorns, and the thorns sprang up with it and choked it. But others fell on good ground, sprang up, and yielded a crop a hundredfold.

Jesus clearly explains the parable as the seed being the Word of God in our hearts. The first seed fell by the wayside are the ones that hear the Word, but then the devil comes and takes the Word out of their hearts and keeps them from faith in the Word to be saved. The rocky soil is those that don't have deep roots; they believe for each season but fail to endure when they face temptations. The seed that fell in the thorns are they that hear but give in to the world's cares and pleasures. Jesus is clearly illustrating the need to guard your heart with the Word of God. Allow the Word to fall in the good rich ground to bring forth fruit in its season.

It didn't take long for me to encounter this enemy the Lord told us would come with the purpose to steal the Word from our hearts. I immediately experienced the fight of faith in my life and learned how to keep the truth in my heart. Sometimes it took years to overcome places, but through God's faithfulness and grace, I have overcome. The enemy does attack, and his sole purpose is to do as Jesus said, steal, kill, and destroy. After my salvation, I thought that things would be way better in life, and I didn't have to concern myself with troubles anymore because I have found the love of Jesus. Well, that is a two-sided situation. Yes, my salvation brought everlasting joy and victory, but that doesn't mean I would no longer go through the suffering and pain in this world. In this world, Jesus said we would have troubles, but to be in good cheer because He has overcome the world (John 16:33). The sufferings and trials continue in this world; it's just now we are positioned as believers in Christ and have the victory in our Lord and Savior who has overcome it all. That doesn't mean we are immune to pain and difficulty.

GUARD YOUR HEART AGAINST FEAR

God's Word tells us that He has not given us the spirit of fear, but a power, love, and a sound mind. Fear is a thief that comes to destroy your peace. When we are tempted to be afraid, we have to resist every lie that tries to dominate our emotions and thoughts. Fear is a liar. It is not the truth. When fear comes, you have to let the love of God respond. It's so important to resist fear in every way. Once you allow a little fear in, you will begin to have a mindset that is contrary to the mind of Christ. It will keep stealing your victory. The only way to stop anxious thoughts is not to tolerate them. Your Heavenly Father said He has not given you a spirit of fear, but power, love, and a *sound mind*. Any thoughts that steal your clarity and focus and put you in a loop of what ifs are not from your Heavenly Father. You must believe in every Word your Father has spoken to you, and you must trust that His plans and purposes are good, and you have to keep your hope that no matter what you face, your Heavenly Father will see you through.

I remember being consumed with fear when my son was fighting for his life. The what ifs kept replaying in my mind endlessly. It was terrible. It was a fearful situation. But what I wasn't trusting or seeing was God's faithfulness, even in a tragedy, His steadfast love that would keep my heart free from fear of what ifs. Once I decided to trust God with the outcome despite the pain it would cost me, fear lost its power over me and our situation. When fear comes, let the love of God respond. Standing on the sure foundation of a Father's love will keep you from the enemy of fear that comes to steal your peace and destroy your destiny. Our Father longs for us to trust Him and believe His Word is true. We must give all our hearts to loving and believing the Father in all things. When we walk in love, we walk in agreement with our Heavenly Father because it is who he is, love. 1 John 4:16 (KJV) *And we have known and believed the love that God hath to us. God is love; and he that dwelleth in love dwelleth in God, and God in him.* When we allow fear to come in, we are not in line with our Father's love and purpose.

It took me many years to understand that we have a daily choice to walk in the empowerment of God's love or walk in the constant battling of fear. You cannot walk in love and fear at the same time. Either love or fear will be getting your attention and devotion. 1 John 4:18 (NIV) *There is no fear in love; but perfect love drives out fear: because fear has to do with punishment. The one who fears is not made perfect in love.* You need to choose to believe in the power of the love of God, to overcome fear, and restore your mind to peace. Choose life. Do not allow a defeated foe of fear to rob you of your God-given right of peace of mind. Knowing your Father's love will ensure you of his plans and purposes are good. So, anything contrary to that is not from your Father. Fear will come, and it will try to intimidate you to get you to believe its report contrary to God's Word.

Jesus tells us that my sheep hear my voice and the voice of a stranger they will not follow (John 10). As a child of God, the voice of fear is a stranger to you because Christ has not given it to you, so resist to follow it, or believe it, and certainly do not be led by it. Let the love of God's victory over the enemy be your guide and light.

Submit yourselves, then, to God. Resist the devil, and he will flee from you (James 4:7, NIV).

GUARD YOUR HEART AGAINST DOUBT

Anytime you are wrestling with fear, doubt will accompany it. Doubt is another device of the enemy to rob you of the Father's love. Doubt is an evil lie that comes to steal your hope and faith. It will cause you to fall into unbelief. God's Word tells us it is impossible to please God without faith. Hebrews 11:6, NIV, *And without faith it is impossible to please God, because anyone who comes to him must believe that he exists and that he rewards those who earnestly seek him.* Our Father wants our wholehearted trust. He wants us to know Him and believe that what He said is true and trust Him. Doubt causes you to waiver in a double mind. Scripture says a doubleminded man is unstable in all his ways. James 1:6-8, NIV, *But when you ask, you must believe and not doubt, because the one who doubts is like a wave of the sea, blown and tossed by the wind. That person should not expect to receive anything from the Lord. Such a person is double-minded and unstable in all they do.* Why is he unstable? Because he doesn't believe! He has no direction. He is uncertain. Our Father's love doesn't leave us wondering; He has given us a clear direction. He is certain. We can know that doubt does not come from God at all. Have you ever needed to make an important decision and instantly knew the direction to go but started to doubt it? You prayed and believed this was the way or answer, but you pulled back and began to question if this is the right decision? That wavering took place and stole your direction, your certainty, and your trust that the Father was directing you. I am not talking about when you are praying about something and discerning God's voice and will. I am talking about when you know you heard and know your Father's will, but doubt comes to cause you to question. Our Father has not given us that doubt; he does not leave us wondering, he doesn't want us in a place of uncertainty. He wants us to trust in Him and follow His truth.

When we pray for anything according to his will, we must believe and receive His faithfulness is sure. Hebrews 11:1, KJV, scripture says that, "Now faith is the substance of things hoped for, the evidence of the things unseen." That means faith is confident in what we hope for from our Heavenly Father's love; even when we do not see it, we can believe it and trust that God is faithful all the time. His purpose will always remain the same to bring us into a future and a hope.

The enemy will use doubt to cause you to stumble in unbelief and distrust, to steal the Word of truth from your heart. Because he knows that if you truly discover the truth, you will be set free, you will overcome, and God's perfect purpose will be produced in your life. Think of the parable we talked about at the beginning of this chapter, the parable of the seed. The good soil brought forth a great harvest; that great harvest is what the enemy is after. He wants to prevent the harvest of

God's blessings from producing in your life and the lives of others.

Submit yourselves, then, to God. Resist the devil, and he will flee from you (James 4:7, NIV).

GUARD YOUR HEART FROM DISAPPOINTMENTS

Learning to guard your heart from disappointments is vital to walking in the fullness of your relationship with the Lord. It took me years to discover the need to guard my heart against disappointments. The truth is, they will come. In this world, Jesus told us we would have troubles, have trails, and suffer. But Jesus also told us to have faith because he has overcome the world (John 16:33, paraphrased). This is a tough thing to understand and a very hard things to walk out. But I assure you when you learn to cast your cares on Christ because He cares for you, you will overcome the difficulties of disappointments. Have you ever put your hope and faith into something, you believed and prayed, and you knew the will of God, and yet it did not prevail? This can be a devastating feeling. Hope deferred makes the heart sick (Proverbs 13:12, paraphrased). The disappointment can crush your spirit, and it can cause you to fall into a place of depression. When you were let down in place of fellow believers I have experienced, I understand the devastation that can afflict your soul. It can leave you with a great wound. You did everything right, committed, dedicated, walked out your faith, prayed, interceded, fasted, pleaded, and yet the situation did not change; God's purposes was not achieved. Instead, the enemy seemed to win; divisions, hurt, broken relationships, distrust in leadership, and everything contrary seemed to occur. Great disappointments have taken place. The first thing the enemy will do is use the pain of trauma to afflict your heart of trust and belief. You will find yourself in a spin cycle of agitation unless you immediately release the disappointment to the Father. I know because I have walked through that season for many years, I learned to guard my heart against it.

In some cases, it can take years away from you; before you know it, several years have passed, and yet the disappointment of that season is still lingering in your soul and hindering you from walking in your next season of victory. You are replaying that disappointment from the past, and whether you realize it or not, you are expecting the disappointment to retake place. The word disappointment will continually dis-appoint you every season until you learn how to surrender every injustice to the Father's love. We must respond to the disappointments with the Father's love. We have to realize there is an enemy at work, and he is working against God's purposes. Not every disappointment is appointed. God's will is something that everyone has the free will to choose. God doesn't force people to choose Him;

He gives them a choice. When you have done all you can do, you have to stand on the Father's love. Never stop believing and praying, but guard your heart against the weight of disappointment, and trust the Father of restoration to bring restoration and completion to all areas of your life. Remember the Word of your Father, everything that was meant for evil God will turn it around and use it for good. Romans 8:28 (NIV) *And we know that in all things God works for the good of those who love him, who have been called according to his purpose.* You need to fully trust that God will use all the injustices, disappointments, and hardships for your good.

Resist the place of disappointment and cast your care on Christ because he cares for you.

GUARD YOUR HEART FROM OFFENSE AND UNFORGIVENESS

When dealing with disappointments, you will be tempted to be offended. Offenses will come. Jesus told us that. How we handle, it is the crucial part. We must allow the Father's love to respond to the offense. God has instructed us how to deal with it, and he said if your brother sins against you, go to them in private and handle the ought. If he hears you, you won back your brother. If he doesn't bring two or three witnesses. When Peter asked Lord how many times must, I forgive my brother, seven times? Jesus responded not seven times but seven times seventy times (Matthew 18, paraphrase).

There is no limit on the love of the Father for reconciliation and forgiveness. The Father's love is to restore, forgive, and reconcile. The enemy will continually use the trap of offense to derail you from fulfilling the Father's purpose in your life. Your heavenly Father's will is the forgiveness of sins, restoration in our relationship with Him and one another. When we choose unforgiveness, grudges, and bitterness towards one another, it is the exact opposite of your Heavenly Father's character, nature, and will for our lives. We must forgive, reconcile, and walk in the Father's love in our relationships with one another. Jesus told us to love one another just as I have loved you (John 13: 24, paraphrased). Jesus told us it was by our love for one another the world would know we were His disciples, not just any love but the love of God (John 13:35, paraphrased). The love that heals delivers and restores humanity into the perfect image of the son. The love that reflects the nature and beauty of God, the love that sanctifies us, satisfies us and calls us His own. This love overcomes all the offenses of this world.

This love and forgiveness are not something we can do within our strength; we need the Father's love, the Father's power, the Father's forgiveness to operate through us in the moments of offense. It is a choice. We can surrender the offense to the Father's love and allow His forgiveness to not only heal but mend every broken place. When I think of the body of Christ, the scripture tells us how we need one another. The eye can't say unto the hand I don't need you and cut it off (1 Corinthians 12:21, paraphrased). There is no brokenness in Christ's body. We are fully and securely fit together as a perfect unity, with Christ being our head. We need one another; we need to walk in one accord, according to His Word. His love will mend us together, keep us together, and heal us together when we allow the Father's love to operate through every offense and division the enemy tries to sow. Unforgiveness is never the plan of the Father; Jesus warned us in Matthew 18 that if we don't forgive one another that we will not be forgiven. God's plan is the forgiveness of all sin for everyone. That is who He is, and when we walk in a way that isn't reflecting his love, we are not walking in His ways. The enemy will try to get you into a place of offense to keep you from walking in the liberty of the Father's love. 1 Peter 4:8 NIV *Above all, love each other deeply, because love covers over a multitude of sins.* The Father's love is great enough to cover all our sins, and we should never hold unforgiveness knowing the Father's love.

Resist the enemy of offense, reflect the Father's love of total forgiveness and restoration.

THE RENEWING OF YOUR MIND

The enemy's number one target is your mind. If he can infiltrate your thinking, he can penetrate your heart. The Lord has given us victory over the enemy in every way; through the death, burial, and resurrection of Christ, the enemy is defeated. But that doesn't mean the enemy has stopped operating; he still has his purpose and plan to kill, steal, and destroy. Jesus clearly described how the seed of God's Word is planted, and then how the enemy comes to take it away. God has done His part and will continue to be faithful and true. Our role is to align our lives with His Word. In my early years of walking with the Lord, I realized that there were a lot of battles I had lost because of my lack of knowledge. Scripture says we are destroyed because of the lack of knowledge (Hosea 4:6, paraphrased). My Father has faithfully shown me through trial and error how to overcome, discern, and keep the victory.

For the weapons of our warfare are mighty to pull down the strongholds (2 Corinthians 10:4, paraphrased). God has given us His weapons, and His weapons are mighty. We must put on the full armor of God every day. We must be diligent in soberness, like the Bible tells us. It says be sober, vigilant because your enemy is roaring around like a lion seeking whom he may devour (1 Peter 5:8, paraphrased). The armor of God is the finished work of Christ. Fully complete. But if we don't exercise it, if we don't put it on, we don't' renew our minds according to the Word, we may fall prey to the enemy. I encourage my kids all the time to discern knowing the difference between, what is God's part, and what is your part. We have a part in this, we have walking out of our faith and due diligence to be alert and ready.

When I discovered the vital importance of renewing my mind according to the Word, I realized the Word was the way of truth to discern every lie of the enemy. I realized the mighty weapon it is against the attacks of the enemy. I learned to rightfully divide the Word of truth and put my mind on it. Philippians 4:8 (paraphrased) tells us to think about these things, whatsoever is true, whatsoever things are honest, just, pure, lovely, and good reports. When we put our minds on the truth of God's love, we overcome every lie. Our Father has overcome the enemy of our souls by sending us his son Jesus, and when we receive and believe in the finished work of cavalry, we are transformed into the sons and daughters of God. Our Father's love, nature, and life are living on the inside of us. Our Father is truth itself, and when we truly know the truth, it will set us free.

We must stay committed to the truth of God's Word that reveals his love, nature, and purpose. Jesus said that His sheep hear His voice; our lives must continually be filled with the voice of truth through his Word. It is so vital to walk in the victory that God has for you. If you neglect to reflect on the truth, it will be easier for the enemy to deceive you. If you put your mind on the truth and obey God's Word with all your heart, His Word is a safeguard from every enemy along the way. Joshua 1:8 (paraphrased) instructs us that we are to meditate day and night and be careful to do what the Word says, and in that, we will find success.

The renewing of our mind is so critical for a healthy, complete life in Christ. Without it, we walk as an unarmed target for the enemy to steal the Word of truth from your heart. Psalms 119:9-12 (NIV) *How can a young person stay on the path of purity? By living according to your word. I seek you with all my heart; do not let me stray from your commands. I have hidden your word in my heart that I might not sin against you. Praise be to you, Lord; teach me your decrees.* God has given us all we need to succeed, and it is all in his Word. He is a faithful Father, and our part is to believe His Word is true and obey it with all our hearts. We can trust that His Word will never return void. Even in the darkest valleys, His Word will always be a light to your path. When we allow His Word to be our priority in life, we will be successful because we live according to the firm foundation of a Father's Love.

OBEY GOD'S WORD

We need to fully understand the importance of obeying God's Word with our whole hearts. Just as your earthly father longs for your obedience, how much more does your heavenly Father longs for your obedience. Scripture tells us that even Jesus learned obedience through the things He suffered. Hebrews 5:8 (KJV) *Though He were a Son, yet learned He obedience by the things which He suffered; And being made perfect, He became the author of eternal salvation unto all them that obey Him.* In the same way, we need to walk in obedience to Christ. Obedience keeps you in perfect alignment with your Heavenly Father's purpose and will. Remember, He has a future and a hope for you in His plans, but we have to be willing to obey Him, seek Him, and commit to following Him.

Our obedience is not out of a religious duty to earn anything with God. Our obedience is out of our pure hearted devotion to our Heavenly Father. Even Jesus said, if you love me, you will obey me (John 14:15, paraphrased). It can be easy to get sidetracked in our walks with God by focusing on areas of great faith and not enough focus on the simple commandments of Christ that call us to obey. In Luke 17:6, KJV, *"And the Lord said, 'If ye had faith as a grain of mustard seed, ye might say unto this sycamine tree, Be thou plucked up by the root, and be thou planted in the sea; and it should obey you.'"* Jesus says faith as small as a mustard seed, could uproot a tree could it be that our obedience is the mustard seed faith? What we think of as small and insignificant is extremely powerful. It the small things that matter. Most read this scripture and see the power displayed, and long for that, they focus on the power and the faith. But genuine faith takes trust and obedience. I have seen it happen in my own life and others; we believe in God, but we don't see the benefits of our faith operate in our lives. What is missing? Our obedience. Don't overlook the simplicity of our relationship in Christ. If we fail to walk in whole-hearted devotion to the commands of Christ to love one another, how can we expect our faith to move trees and mountains? When we are unwilling to allow that same faith to change our very own hearts towards one another? We are called to love God, love people, and live holy. God wants us to walk in obedience to his Word in all ways. Why? Because He wants you to live your best life, the life He designed for you. When we get caught up in offenses, bitterness, gossip, slander, divisions, and discords, it is not pleasing to our Heavenly Father. He gave all he had so that that sin nature would no longer dominate us, He gave us His son and His spirit a renewed man, a restored mind, a recreated heart, an image that reflects His love and glory. His life now empowers us to bear the fruit of his righteousness. These things matter to the heart of our Father. He wants us to walk in His ways to reflect His love.

It is important to obey our Father in all things, not some things, or a select few, but in all. When we truly love the Father, our hearts will long to obey Him. He will help us in every way. He has given us the helper, the comforter, to lead us in the way of life. He will be our strength, our guide, our comfort, and our direction. In so many seasons, I spent countless hours seeking God's will in prayer and turning to His holy Word for the direction that I needed. We must come to Him in humility, in repentance, in pure devotion, and with a heart just longing for Him. He is faithful; He is true; we can trust His Word will prevail when we set our lives to obey Him in all we do. Lord, every day let us walk in complete obedience to your Word, to believe you, trust you, love you, love others, and reflect your glory in all we do.

CHAPTER 10

Reflecting the Father's Love

Let's revisit the beginning of this journey. I started by sharing how our lives are a lot like houses, and every house needs a strong foundation. The foundation of every life is a Father's love. Without a father, there would be no life, no start, no beginning. Our Heavenly Father's love is our firm foundation. His great love is revealed to us by sending His only begotten Son Jesus to reconcile us to a relationship with Himself. In 2 Corinthians 5:18-19 (NIV) the Word of God says, *All this is from God, who reconciled us to Himself through Christ and gave us the ministry of reconciliation; that God was reconciling the world to Himself in Christ, not counting people's sins against them. And He has committed to us the message of reconciliation.* Our lives are reconstructed and completely rebuilt to reflect the glory of His love. Our Father has fully redeemed our lives to reflect His perfect nature and love. Through faith in Jesus Christ, the only begotten Son of

God, we are raised to new life and transformed from the inside out, not outside in.

The day I received Jesus as my savior, was the day everything in me changed. I was raised to a new life by God's spirit. Only God could heal and restore the broken foundation in my life. He set my new life upon a sure foundation that will never fail, His love. We all are like houses, we all have a foundation, and maybe your life wasn't like mine, filled with the brokenness of abuse and addiction, but you are still in the same need I am, a Father's love. Everyone is born into sin, the fall of humanity, and we all need to be restored to our Heavenly Father through Christ our Lord and Savior.

BORN AGAIN

But as many as received Him, to them gave he the power to become the sons of God even to them that believe on His name, which were born not of blood nor of the will of flesh nor of the will of man, But of God.

John 1:12 (KJV)

The change happened from the inside out. My heart changed, my desires changed, my mind changed, I had only one desire, and that was to live my life free in the love of God. I was no longer shackled by the chains of sin, or the prison of my sinful desires. My desires changed from darkness to light. I wanted to do what was right because of the great love that healed my life. When I believed and received the love of God it changed me entirely.

In the book of John chapter three, a religious leader named Nicodemus came to Jesus seeking to learn more about God, He knew Jesus was from God because of the miracles Jesus performed. Jesus told Nicodemus that no one can see the kingdom of God unless you are born again. Nicodemus could not understand, how a man could go back into his mother's womb? Jesus explained that being born again comes from the Spirit of God, not your mother's womb. To be born again is the will of God for all mankind.

At the foot of the cross of Calvary we come to a place of divine exchange; we surrender our lives for the life of Christ. Jesus told us in Mark 8:34-36 (NIV) *"Whoever wants to be my disciples must deny themselves and take up their cross and follow me. For whoever wants to save their life will lose it, but whoever loses their life for me and for the gospel will save it. What good is it for someone to gain the whole world, yet forfeit their soul?"* I realized the life I was living was no life at all, I surrendered all of me to gain all of Christ. To live born again is to be raised in new life, the old has passed away, we are created new in Christ. Our entire lives can be made brand new from the inside out, not the outside in. All we simply need to do is receive, believe, and become all that our Heavenly Father has created us to be, which is his sons.

RECONSTUCTING THE HOUSE

Every house goes through a building process, and when we come into the new life of Christ, our foundation is new! The Lord then begins a reconstructing process in our lives. I shared a lot of my journey with you to how the Lord rebuilt my life. It took a great deal of time, and there is a lot of process I went through in understanding my Father's love and will continue to go through until the day we are with him face to face. Life is a journey, and it takes time to develop. Just as an infant has stages and seasons of growth, so do we in our new life. We need time to grow into full maturity. A lot of my growth came by trial and error. I cannot count the countless times I missed it or needed to go through the same lessons a time or two. But in each season, the Father was establishing my life even more in His love. Sometimes the building process can be painful because there are things that need to be removed. But in our Father's love, we can be ensured that it is for our good.

We must embrace and endure through the process. I often cried rivers of tears, asking the Lord, why am I going through a particular storm again? I don't understand. It wasn't until I got through the valley that I could see the purpose of the journey. It was to build my life even more upon His never-failing love. I learned to trust the process that we need to go through and allow His love to guide me every step of the way through the darkest valleys. The one great lesson I learned is never to give up. Never give up in the process of reconstructing, endure, and embrace the journey of being made for His glory. It will be difficult, there is no doubt about that, but the reward is so great. There will be times when you take a step back, and you can catch a beautiful glimpse of the restoration of the house your Father is building out of your life, and you will say the pain I have endured cannot compare to the joy that is to come. So, keep building with your Heavenly Father, allow Him to repair, restore, and reconstruct your life upon His love; even when it gets difficult, do not give up because He is making something beautiful in you a reflection of His love.

CALLED TO REFLECT OUR FATHER'S LOVE

Jesus said to him, "Have I been with you so long, and yet you have not known me, Philip? He who has seen Me has seen the Father; so how can you say, 'Show us the Father?' Do you not believe that I am in the Father, and the Father in Me? The words that I speak to you I do not speak on My own authority; but the Father who dwells in Me does the works, Believe Me that I am in the Father and the

Father in Me, or else believe Me for the sake of the works themselves.

John 14:9-11 (NKJV)

Through my process, I realized that the most significant project God was building in me was His character and nature of His love. Through all the hardships, trails, and places, I realized God wanted me to reflect Him in all my ways. Jesus told us, if you see me, you have seen the Father, the Father is in me, and I am in the Father. How amazing! Jesus reflected the Father's love in everything because the Father and He are one. Jesus also told us that He does not do or say anything unless He hears or sees the Father do it. Jesus's life was entirely built on the Father's love and is the perfect reflection of the Father's image and heart in everything He did. A true son reflects the character and nature of their Father. That is who Jesus is, the only begotten Son of God! Jesus's purpose was to reveal His Father to us and restore us to the Father through Him!

We are now through Jesus called to that same reflection of love. As a child of God, we are called to reflect His nature in all we do. The greatest calling, we have is to be a child of God and reflect the Father's love in Jesus. The scripture tells us the characteristics of a child of God. The Father has established your foundation, your identity, your purpose, and your character is a reflection of

His love. Jesus told us that by the fruit, you know a tree. Matthew 7:17-18, NLT, *A good tree produces good fruit, and a bad tree produces bad fruit, A good tree can't produce bad fruit, and a bad tree can't produce good fruit.* We are known by what we produce, and by being born again and raised to the new life of Christ, we become a good tree! A good tree brings forth good fruit! Remember when I told you the change is from the inside out, not the outside in? A tree cannot put on good fruit and dress in something that it is not producing from its roots. Therefore, it is important to have your roots grounded in the new life of Christ, not just your words or your effort of trying to be "good." A relationship with God is not born out of you trying to be "good," we know there is no "good" but God. You must receive and believe He is good and surrender your old life, the bad tree, for the new life in Christ, the good tree. To produce the fruit and reflection of the Father's love. Apart from Jesus, we cannot produce good fruit, remember He is the vine, and we are the branches. It is His life that produces good fruit in us.

As a child of God, he replaces, restores, and removes the old life with his new life of Christ. The Word of God instructs us to put off the old man corrupted by lust and deception (Ephesians 4:22, paraphrase). Instead, put on the new man that is created according to God in righteousness and holiness (Ephesians 4:24, paraphrase). This is all a part of the growth process we go through, with walking in new life and relationship with our Father's love. We learn to every day choose to follow Christ, live according to His will, and surrender to His life. When we daily choose to allow God to be glorified in our lives, we are constantly renewed and walking in a redemptive life. All the while, we are in a relationship, our daily choices and actions reflect His great love. Jesus said in Matthew 16:24, NKJV, *"If anyone desires to come after Me, let him deny himself, and take up his cross and follow Me."*

AM I REFLECTING MY FATHER'S LOVE?

In every decision, in every situation, in every relationship, in every season, in every difficulty, I have begun to ask myself, "Am I reflecting my Father's love." We learn that living is all about surrendering to the Father's will. The best life we can live is a life submitted to the Holy Father. Jesus, Himself in the garden, cried out, "Not my will be done, but yours be done, Father."

We are called to that same high calling, of denying ourselves, picking up our cross, following Christ in everything and everyway. As a mature son, we learn that we follow the image and likeness of our Father, and His purpose and will is established in our lives. Many times, the purpose will cause pain and suffering, just as it did for Jesus. He suffered, for our sins, and paid the highest cost. But He trusted the Father with it all. He sacrificed His life so that the Father's love would be revealed to all mankind. Jesus was devoted to the Father's purpose and will because Jesus is the perfect reflection of His Father's love. His very life was in the Father, the Father in Him, and He is the Father, a perfect unity of relationship.

Jesus trusted the Father with the pain, and He trusted the Father with His justification. He trusted the Father with his resurrection! He trusted His Father with everything. When the night came for Jesus's betrayal, He reflected the Father's love in all His ways. When his closest friends slept instead of prayed, denied instead of defended, betrayed instead of protected, when everyone turned away, He still chose the Father's love. He loved us all every step of the way. He restored the soldier's ear that was cut off, and He gave even then the Father's love. When He was whipped and beaten, they mocked Him and accused Him, when they yelled terrible things. They cried out, crucify Him, crucify Him! When there was no blame, He was a spotless lamb tender in love, who only wanted to reflect the Father's love. They placed the crown of thorns on His head, mocked and beat him for a crime he did not commit.

All in all, He walked in the Father's great love. They pierced His hands and nailed His feet to a cross that would bleed the spotless Holy lamb of God's blood for all mankind. He did not deserve any of the punishment he received. He only wanted to reflect His Father's love. He steadfastly went and willingly laid His life down so that we would all see the gracious love of a Father that longs for us to be free. When He thirsted, they did not give Him a drink, He who gave His all, so that we would be free. They ripped His clothing from Him and hung Him on a tree for us to all see. All the while, He reflected His Father's love and still did not condemn one but called us only to believe the Father had sent Him so that we would be free. In every way, Jesus reflected the Father's love, as He laid down His life perfect and free, to pay a price that was owed by you and me. In all the mistreatment and all the abuse, He still cried out, "Father forgive them, for they do not know what they do." He chose to reflect His Father's, great Love. As He took His last breath, He spoke that it was finished and that it was complete. Jesus Christ, the only begotten Son of God, had revealed to us His great Father's love.

This is the life of the only begotten Son that reflected His Father's love so that we can too today become His sons. I am free for the sacrifice my Savior made, to pay the price that I could never pay. In every injustice, in every betrayal, in every hurt, in every way, Lord give me the strength to be like you and pray, "Father not my will but yours be done, and make me a reflection of your great love." Jesus called us to one thing, and that is to live holy and free. He called us to be like Him, reflecting the Father's love.

Jesus said,

"As the Father loved Me, I also have loved you, abide in My love. If you keep my commandments, you will abide in My love, just as I have kept My Father's commandments and abide in His love. These things I have spoken to you, that My joy may remain in you, and that your joy may be full. This is My commandment, that you love one another as I have loved you. Greater love has no one than this, than to lay down one's life for his friends. You are My friends if you do whatever I command you. No longer do I call you servants, for a servant does not know what his master is doing; but I have called you friends, for all things that I heard from My Father I have made known to you. You did not choose Me, but I chose you and appointed you that you should go and bear fruit, and that your fruit should remain, that whatever you ask the Father in my name He may give you. These things I command you, that you love one another."

John 15:11-17 (NKJV)

The End.